MEDITERRANEAN
Lifestyle
COOKING

THE KEY TO A HEALTHY LIFE THROUGH SIMPLE AND DELICIOUS COOKING

MEDITERRANEAN
Lifestyle
COOKING

THE KEY TO A HEALTHY LIFE THROUGH SIMPLE AND DELICIOUS COOKING

Mary Valle

NH
NEW HOLLAND

CONTENTS

DEDICATION

For Steven, Catherine, Rebecca and Sarah

INTRODUCTION

My first kitchen was small, did not have the latest oven or any stylish gadgets. The pantry was tiny and there was not a lot of cupboard space. The bench had enough room for a toaster and, like my mother, I too would have a small Greek Orthodox icon sitting in a corner, where I would light a small candle on special days. My one indulgence was a bouquet of fresh flowers, usually roses as they are my favorite. The tiles around my kitchen bench were a retro orange, which I grew to love. We had a small rectangular table which usually had one of my mother's hand-embroidered tablecloths on it, four chairs around it and, of course, a child's high chair.

You could not imagine seeing a photograph of this kitchen in the latest design magazines but it was my kitchen, a place where many meals were prepared and many happy memories made. Even though I still have visions of my dream kitchen, I would never change the memories of that small, not very stylish but cosy kitchen.

As a mother, when I look back I want to know that when blessed with this incredible 'job' I did the very best I could, and that for me includes knowing my family eats well. I do confess that there are times when I feel that I have been cooking forever, and that is okay.

For me, home cooking is about dishes that are not complicated or clever but delicious and nutritious in the simplest way … knowing what is in every meal that you have prepared. I cherish the intimacy of the family table, sharing meals you have prepared with love and soul for the people you love.

I have a passion for Mediterranean food and especially Greek food as it is what I know best. Food from the Mediterranean resembles a way of life … meals using the freshest seasonal produce, prepared simply and shared with family and friends.

Food has the ability to stir up many emotions. It can take you back to your childhood, remind you of a special dinner with a special someone or a place that you have visited. The recipes in this book are all meals that I prepare for my family, many favorites. I hope that you make these recipes your own and are not afraid to add a personal touch … have some fun and enjoy!

THE INGREDIENTS OF THE MEDITERRANEAN DIET

Olive oil (the main source of fat)

Herbal teas

Beans and legumes at least twice a week

Fruit everyday for dessert

Vegetables with every meal

Fruit and vegetables that are in season

Enjoy wild greens

Share meals with family and friends at the dinner table

Poultry at least twice a week
Less red meat as a side, or once a week

Fish at least twice a week

Drink water

Alcohol always with a meal and in moderation

Exercise daily

Strong sense of community

Learn to cook

Eat yogurt everyday and cheese in moderation

Herbs and spices instead of salt to season foods

Sweets can be for special occasions

Olive Oil

Olive oil is an integral ingredient and the cornerstone of the Mediterranean diet – an 'everyday food'.

Greece is the world's third largest producer of olive oil and a leader in the consumption of it. Most of the olive oil produced in Greece is used domestically and little is exported, Spain being the largest producer of olive oil and Italy the second.

It is rich in monounsaturated fatty acids and is the main source of dietary fat in the Mediterranean diet. Extra virgin and virgin olive oils have a greater health benefit as they retain the majority of the olive fruit's nutrients, it also contains natural antioxidants such as polyphenols and carotenoids and vitamin E. These antioxidants are a protective agent and there have been many studies into the benefits of its consumption. These studies show that people who consume olive oil regularly reduce their risk of cardiovascular disease and stroke as well as having a protective role towards some cancers developing, such as breast and skin cancers. These studies go even further and suggest additional benefits such as

maintaining a healthy blood pressure, healthy cholesterol levels, immune function, protection against Alzheimer's disease, diabetes, rheumatoid arthritis, osteoporosis, type 2 diabetes, depression and promoting a healthy weight.

To invite the greatest benefits from olive oil always use fresh, usually 18 months to 2 years from harvest. Once a bottle is opened use within 6 months, this should not be a problem if olive oil becomes an everyday food. It is not just for salads, as some would believe; it is also used in all cooking, stewing, braising, roasting and frying (it has a smoke point high enough for home frying needs). Studies have shown, to receive the benefits of olive oil, you need to consume about 45 ml (1 1/2 fl oz) a day, which is not that difficult if you cook with olive oil and use it to dress your salads as well.

There are many varieties of olives, the most important ones being those with a high polyphenol ontent producing a more stable oil. The Koroneiki variety grown mainly in Crete and in the Peleponese is one of the most important varieties, together with Picual and Conicabra varieties from Spain and Coraina and Moraiolo varieties from Italy.

Olive oil not only provides these health benefits and protective factors: it also enhances the taste of our food. It makes food more palatable and easier to digest. Medical studies show that many nutrients are fat-soluble, not water soluble, requiring dietary fat to absorb. Therefore, cooking in olive oil not only heightens the nutrients, but also allows for easier absorption.

Wild Greens

Wild greens are an organic part of the Mediterranean diet. They are packed with nutrients and a great source of vitamins, minerals, antioxidants, source of omega 3 fatty acids and calcium. Wild greens and olive oil are a perfect marriage. Whether they are cooked in olive oil or dressed with it, the oil assists in the development of their fine flavors. Recent studies show that not only is the flavor enhanced but the health benefits of vegetables are also heightened by adding olive oil onto them, as the oil aids in the absorption of the nutrients, therefore providing the greatest benefits.

Amaranth (Amaranth viridis), known as 'vlita' in Greek, is popular in Greece. There are many varieties of amaranth, sometimes cultivated for its seeds.
The leaves are boiled for salads, fillings for pies or used in braises with zucchini, green beans, purslane or potatoes.

Dandelion, known as 'radiki' in Greek, is eaten raw as well as cooked in salads and braises.

Nettles, known as 'tsouknida' in Greek, and are always eaten cooked, mainly as fillings in pies.

Arugula (Rocket) known as 'roka' in Greek is used raw in salads or cooked in braises.

Purslane, also known as 'glistrida',
is used mainly raw in salads.

Wild fennel, known in Greek as 'marathon', is used in salads,
savory pies, fritters and stuffed dishes.

Wild Chicory is known also as 'radiki' in Greek and is boiled
for salads.

Beans and Pulses

Beans and pulses are the foundation of the simple, health-giving Mediterranean cuisine.

Since ancient times, this simple ingredient has been feeding families in an economical and wholesome way. Beans and pulses are low in fat, rich in antioxidants and high in fibre, and are an excellent source of protein, which assists in the protection against heart disease, diabetes and some cancers.

Beans and lentils are also an excellent source of iron. The most popular being white beans such as cannellini and butter beans, chickpeas, lentils, black-eyed peas and yellow split peas. They are mashed, baked, added to soups, casseroles and salads and also made into fritters.

As a young girl growing up in a Greek household I remember every Wednesday and Friday beans were on the menu, usually a soup. Whether it was a lentil soup or a white bean soup (fasolada), it was a loyal tradition.

Herbal Teas

Herbal teas provide not only a comforting drink but also have been known for their healing properties according to myths and traditions.

Greek Mountain Shepherds tea (sideritis) has an earthy taste, and using the flowers adds a comforting floral fragrance. This tea is enormously popular in Greece and one that brings back childhood memories, as it was my mother's most loved tea.

Mediterranean families use herbal teas as their remedy for illness, providing aid in times of need from curing colds, respiratory ailments, digestion, assisting the immune system, to calming mild anxiety and as an antioxidant. Sage tea (faskomilo) and Camomile are used for calmness. Linden (tilio) eases coughs and colds and aids in digestion and calming. Oregano (rigani) aids coughs and chest colds.

Herbal teas are easy to prepare. Boil some water, turn off the heat and submerge the dried herbs, cover and allow to rest for a few minutes. Strain and drink with or without honey.

PANTRY

Olive oil
Everyday cooking oil and for salads.

Rice
For paella - short grain rice. There is one called 'bomb' which is great but you can also use short or medium grain rice.

Risotto rice - I like to use Carnaroli.

Medium grain rice - for sweets and stuffings.

Basmati rice or long grain - for pilau.

Pasta
Fresh and dry (fresh keeps for only a fe days in the refrigerator) spaghetti, penne, angel hair and any other variety that you love.

Bread

Grains
Semolina, couscous, bulghur.

Tomato passata, tomato paste and cans of diced tomatoes

Flour
Self-raising (self-rising), plain and Tipo 00.

Yoghurt
I recommend Greek yoghurt, but any natural, creamy yoghurt will do.

Pulses
Lentils, cannellini beans (both dried and in cans), chickpeas (garbanzo beans)

Vanilla extract

Vinegar

Red wine, white wine and balsamic.

Sea salt

Black peppercorns and a grinder

Sugar

Organic, caster (superfine) and icing (confectioners').

Filo pastry

Olives

Cheese

Feta, mozzarella, fresh ricotta, parmigiano.

Honey

Eggs (organic)

Garlic, onions, lemons, potatoes

Dried herbs and spices

Basil, bay leaves, cinnamon (ground and sticks), cloves (ground and whole), fennel seeds, nutmeg, oregano, rosemary, saffron, sesame seeds, sweet paprika, tarragon.

SMALL PLATES

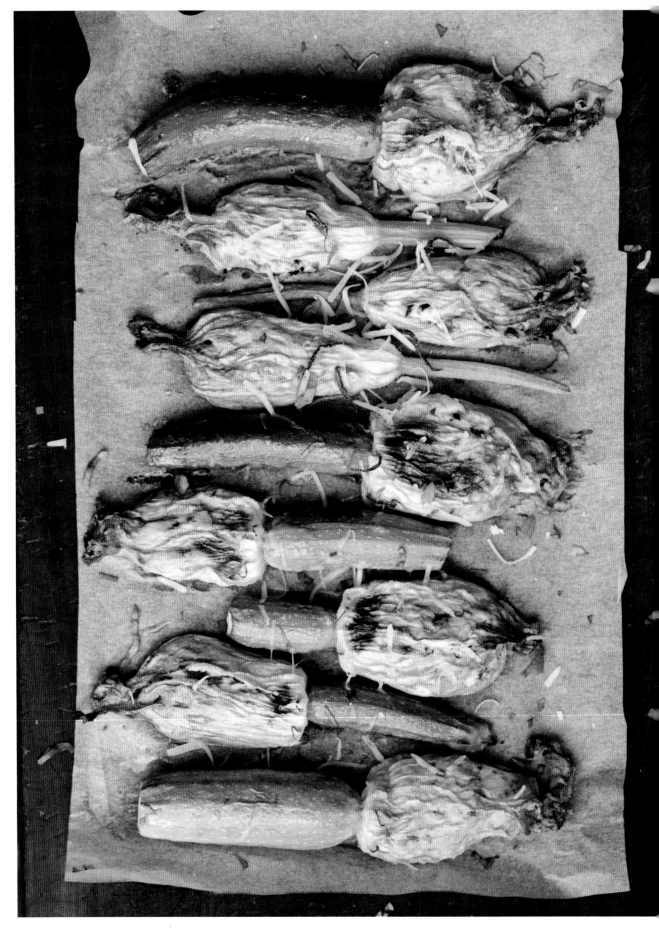

STUFFED ZUCCHINI FLOWERS

Serves 4 to 6

Ingredients

16–20 zucchini (courgette) flowers

1 onion, finely chopped

200 g (7 oz) rice

2 ripe tomatoes, grated

parsley, finely chopped, to taste

dill, finely chopped, to taste

pinch of dried oregano

60 ml (2 fl oz) olive oil

salt, to taste

freshly ground pepper

Method

Preheat the oven to 180°C (350°F).

Prepare the zucchini flowers, rinsing and carefully removing the stamen.

In a frying pan heat the olive oil and sauté the onion until soft. Add the rice and mix well coating the rice with the olive oil and about 120 ml (4 fl oz) of water. Add the tomatoes, herbs and season to taste. Simmer for 3–4 minutes and allow it to cool for a bit.

Place a spoonful of the mixture carefully into each zucchini flower and fold tops over. Arrange in a baking dish. When all finished drizzle a little extra olive oil over and pour 120 ml (4 fl oz) of water into the baking dish.

Bake for about 20–30 minutes or until cooked. You may need to add more water to the baking dish if it is looking too dry.

Serve warm or at room temperature.

Santorini Tomato Rissoles

Serves 4

Ingredients

6 large tomatoes, peeled, seeded and finely diced

1 small brown onion, peeled and grated

small handful parsley, chopped

small handful mint, chopped

1 teaspoon sugar

20 ml (2/3 fl oz) tomato paste

salt and pepper, to taste

200 g (7 oz) plain flour

olive oil

Method

In a large bowl, place the tomato, onion, parsley, mint, sugar, tomato paste and season with salt and pepper. Mix everything together then add the flour. Combine well and the mixture should resemble a batter. In a large frying pan, heat some olive oil, about 2.5 cm (1 in) deep.

Spoon out some of the tomato mixture and carefully place in the pan to deep-fry. Turn over once only. Each side should take only 2–3 minutes or until golden brown.

Continue until all the mixture has been cooked. Remove and drain on some absorbent paper.

Serve immediately. Perfect on a meze platter.

DOLMADES FILLED WITH BULGUR WHEAT

Serves 4 to 6

Ingredients

500 g (1 lb) vine leaves (preserved in jars, these are already blanched)

1 small onion, diced

250 g (9 oz) bulgur wheat

100 g (3 1/2 oz) sultanas or currants

100 g (3 1/2 oz) pine nuts

10 g (1/3 oz) fresh mint, finely chopped

10 g (1/3 oz) fresh parsley, finely chopped

salt, to taste

freshly ground black pepper, to taste

lemon

60 ml (2 fl oz) olive oil

240 ml (8 fl oz) hot water

Avgolemono – egg and lemon sauce (optional, see recipe page 214)

Method

Place the bulgur wheat into a bowl and pour in enough boiling water to cover the bulgur. Cover the bowl and leave for about 20 minutes.

Rinse the vine leaves and trim the stems.

In a frying pan heat the olive oil and sauté the onion, add the prepared bulgur wheat, sultanas, pine nuts, herbs, mix well and season to taste. Take off the heat.

Line a casserole dish with a few vine leaves (use any that have torn or are too small to roll up).

Spoon out 1–2 spoonfuls of the bulgur filling and place at the base of a vine leaf, fold in the sides, roll up and place into the casserole dish. Continue to fill the vine leaves and place them in the dish close together so they keep their shape. When finished drizzle a little extra olive oil over and add 240 ml (8 fl oz) of water. Place a plate upside down onto the dolmades to keep them in place. Cover and simmer for about 20–30 minutes.

If finishing with the egg and lemon sauce prepare it and add it to the dolmades when cooked, removing the dish from the heat and using the liquid the dolmades were cooked in. Shake the dish to distribute the sauce evenly.

You can simply squeeze a lemon over the dolmades if you prefer instead of the egg and lemon sauce. Serve hot.

ZUCCHINI FRITTERS

Serves 4 to 6

Ingredients

olive oil

1 kg (32 oz) zucchini, grated

1 brown onion, grated

3 eggs

handful of parsley, finely chopped

handful of mint, finely chopped

dill, finely chopped, to taste

60 g (2 oz) breadcrumbs

100 g (3 1/2 oz) feta (kefalotiri is also lovely if you prefer)

salt, to taste

freshly ground black pepper

plain flour for coating

lemon

Method

Salt the grated zucchini and place in a sieve to drain for about an hour.
Remove from the sieve and squeeze out any excess liquid and place into a bowl.
Add the grated onion, eggs, herbs, breadcrumbs, feta and season to taste.
Combine well. Rest the mixture in the refrigerator for about an hour.

Heat some olive oil in a large frying pan.
Place some plain flour onto a plate or work surface.
Take enough mixture into your hands, shape into fritters and coat with the flour, shaking off any excess. Fry in the heated olive oil for 4–5 minutes or until golden, turning once. Place on absorbent towels and continue cooking fritters in small batches. Do not overcrowd the frying pan.

Serve with a squeeze of lemon.

CHICKPEA FRITTERS

Serves 4 to 6

Ingredients

30 ml (1 fl oz) olive oil, plus extra for frying

500 g (1 lb) chickpeas (soaked overnight in salted water, 4 teaspoons salt)

1 onion, grated

4 teaspoon mint, finely chopped

4 teaspoon dill, finely chopped

150 g (5 oz) plain flour

2 large ripe tomatoes, grated

1/2 teaspoon sweet paprika

salt, to taste

freshly ground black pepper

lemon juice to serve

Method

Soak the chickpeas in salted water overnight. Drain and wash the chickpeas well, then using a food processor or wooden spoon mix until it resembles a paste. Add the onion, herbs, tomato, paprika and oil and season well. Add the flour slowly mixing well as you go until the mixture looks like a thick paste. Cover and place in the refrigerator for about one hour to rest.

Heat extra olive oil in a frying pan and add large spoonful of the chickpea mixture, cooking on all sides until golden, about 8–10 minutes. Do not overcrowd the frying pan. Place cooked fritters on absorbent paper while cooking the rest of the mixture.
Arrange fritters on a serving platter and squeeze over a little
lemon juice and serve at room temperature.

Yemista (Stuffed Red Peppers)

Serves 4 as main or 8 as a starter

Ingredients

8 medium-sized red capsicums (peppers)

1 onion, finely chopped or grated

olive oil

700 g (1 1/2 lb) minced beef

1 x 680 ml (22 oz) bottle tomato passata

450 g (15 oz) medium grain rice

parsley, chopped

salt and pepper, to taste

Method

Preheat oven to 200°C (400°F).

Wash the capsicums and slice the tops off . Keep the tops aside.

In a large frying pan, sauté onions in a little olive oil until soft. Add mince and tomato passata and mix well. Add 300 ml (10 oz) water, rice, parsley and season with salt and pepper. Cook for about 5–10 minutes.

Spoon mixture into the peppers, put tops back on and place in a large baking dish. You can lay them down or sit them up; whichever way they fit, it really doesn't matter. Drizzle a little olive oil on them and place in the oven for about an hour or until cooked. You may need a little water in the bottom of the dish.

Serve with a green salad, feta cheese and fresh bread.

SALT COD CROQUETTES

Serves 4 to 6

Ingredients

olive oil

1 kg (approx. 2 lb) salt cod

60 g (2 oz) breadcrumbs

60 g (2 oz) plain flour

lemon

10 g (1/3 oz) dill, finely chopped

10 g (1/3 oz) parsley, finely chopped

salt, to taste

freshly ground black pepper

Method

Prepare the salt cod by removing the skin and cutting it into pieces. Place into a large bowl and cover with cold water. It will need to soak overnight to remove the salt.

Remove the water and drain well. Flake the fish using a fork removing any bones. Place the flaked fish into a bowl with the breadcrumbs, flour and herbs. Add a good squeeze of lemon and season to taste with salt (check to see if it needs it) and pepper. The mixture should be a little soft and not too thick.

In a large frying pan pour enough oil to the depth of 1 cm (1/2 in) and heat. Using a large spoon place carefully into the hot oil a spoonful of the salt cod mixture. Fry on both sides until golden brown and allow it to rest on absorbent paper while cooking the remaining mixture.

Serve immediately with the Butter Bean Skordalia (see recipe page 222).

POTATO CROQUETTES

Serves 4 to 6

Ingredients

1 kg (2 lb) potatoes

2 eggs

125 g (4 oz) grated Parmesan cheese

1 small onion, finely chopped

salt and pepper, to taste

1 teaspoon oregano

10 g (1/3 oz) chopped parsley

2 cloves garlic, finely chopped

flour, for dusting

oil, for frying

Method

Cook the unpeeled potatoes in a large pot of boiling water for about 20–30 minutes, or until soft. Drain carefully and peel when cool.

Place the potatoes into a large bowl and mash well. Add the eggs, Parmesan cheese, onion, oregano, parsley and garlic. Season with salt and pepper.

Using your hands, mix all the ingredients well and shape into small rissoles. My mother likes to make them into an oval shape. Coat the rissoles in a little flour, patting the flour onto them as you go.

Heat some oil in a large frying pan and fry the rissoles in small batches until golden brown and crispy, turning once.

STUFFED ONIONS

Serves 4 to 6

Ingredients

7 red onions

100 ml (3 1/2 fl oz) olive oil

150 g (5 oz) minced beef

100 g (3 1/2 oz) rice

15 g (1/2 oz) parsley, finely chopped

4 large ripe tomatoes, grated

salt, to taste

freshly ground black pepper

100 g (3 1/2 oz) pine nuts

100 g (3 1/2 oz) sultanas

1 lemon

Method

This is also lovely made without the mince, simply leave out the mince and double the quantity of rice.

Peel 6 of the onions and slice lengthways but not all the way through, leaving the onion connected at the base. Place them in a large saucepan of boiling water carefully and cook for about 10–12 minutes or until tender. Drain and put aside to cool.

In a frying pan heat the olive oil and sauté the remaining onion (finely diced) until soft. Add the mince, rice, tomatoes, parsley, pine nuts and sultanas. Season to taste.

Preheat oven to 180°C (350°F). When the onions are cool enough to handle, carefully remove the leaves. Place a leaf into the palm of your hand and put a spoonful of the mixture into it and roll, (similar to making dolmades). Continue until all the leaves have been filled and rolled and placing them into a baking dish packed tightly so they do not unroll. Any leaves that are too small to roll can be added to the baking tray together with any mixture that may be left over. Drizzle olive oil over the onions and pour enough water over to come halfway up the onions, but not covering them. Place a plate on top so they stay in place and bake for about 30–40 minutes or until cooked and golden.

Fried Green Peppers

Serves 4

Ingredients

8 sweet green peppers

60 ml (2 fl oz) olive oil

salt, to taste

4 teaspoons dried oregano

Method

Slice the tops halfway, keeping peppers attached and remove the seeds.
In a frying pan heat the olive oil and add the peppers. Sauté on a high heat turning gently so they are browned on all sides. Remove when cooked and serve with a sprinkling of oregano and salt.
Serve with some fresh bread and feta cheese.

Scrambled Eggs with Tomatoes

Serves 4

Ingredients

6 medium-sized tomatoes

3 tablespoons olive oil

salt and pepper, to taste

½ teaspoon sugar

1 teaspoon oregano

8 eggs

2 spring onions, sliced (optional)

Method

Wash the tomatoes well and dice.

In a large frying pan, heat the olive oil and pour in the tomatoes, stirring well. Season to taste, add sugar and oregano and cook for about 7–10 minutes.

Beat the eggs and slowly pour them into the tomato mixture, stirring until the eggs are cooked.

Serve warm garnished with spring onions, together with some toast and a green salad.

KEFTETHES (MEATBALLS)

Serves 4 to 6

Ingredients

2 thick slices day old bread (crusts removed)

500 g (1 lb) minced beef

2 eggs

1 onion, finely chopped or grated

60 g (2 oz) chopped parsley

4 teaspoons dried oregano

salt and pepper, to taste

plain flour for coating

olive oil for frying

Method

Soak the bread in water, squeeze out excess and crumble.

Mix well with other ingredients; the mixture should be moist. Leave in the fridge for about 1 hour.

Take small pieces of the meat mixture and roll into walnut-sized balls.

Coat in flour and fry in hot olive oil.

Can be served hot or at room temperature.

My mother always liked to grate her onions using a hand held grater instead of chopping and dicing. is is something I also noticed many women doing in Greece.

She did this for her keftethes and most of her casseroles.

ROASTED FETA

Serves 4 to 6

Ingredients

400 g (13 oz) feta cheese, sliced

black pepper

olive oil

1 teaspoon dried oregano

lemon wedges

Method

Preheat oven to 220°C (400°F).

Place foil onto baking tray and put slices of feta cheese on it. Season with pepper. Drizzle oil and sprinkle oregano on top. Fold foil and bake for 10 minutes.

Open the foil carefully and squeeze lemon juice over the cheese. Serve while hot.

BRAISED DANDELION

Serves 4 to 6

Ingredients

1 small bunch dandelion greens (remove tough stems)

60 ml (2 fl oz) olive oil

juice of half a lemon

salt, to taste

freshly ground black pepper, to taste

Method

Wash the dandelion leaves well and remove any tough stems.

Cook the greens in a large pot of salted water until tender, about 6–8 minutes.

Drain the greens, squeeze dry and place in a bowl.

Drizzle the olive oil and the lemon juice over, season with salt and pepper and serve at room temperature.

Green Beans and Amaranth (Vlita) Casserole

Serves 4 to 6

Ingredients

1 kg (32 oz) green beans, trimmed

250 g (8 1/2 oz) amaranth (you could also use dandelion or spinach) washed and roughly chopped

4 potatoes, peeled and cut into chunks

100 ml (3 1/2 fl oz) olive oil

1 onion, finely diced

4 large ripe tomatoes, grated

2 cloves garlic, finely diced

15-20 g (1/2 - 2/3 oz) parsley, finely chopped

4 teaspoons mint leaves, finely chopped

4 teaspoons dill, finely chopped

salt, to taste

freshly ground black pepper

Method

In a large casserole pot heat the olive oil and sauté the onions until soft. Add the garlic and tomatoes and 240 ml (8 fl oz) of water. Allow to simmer for 4–5 minutes. Add the green beans and simmer for a further 10 minutes. Add the potatoes, amaranth leaves and herbs. Season to taste and continue cooking for a further 10–15 minutes or until all the vegetables are tender.

Serve hot or at room temperature with fresh crusty bread and some feta cheese.

Amaranth and Zucchini

Serves 4 to 6

Ingredients

1 bunch amaranth leaves (approx. 1 kg/ 32 oz) roughly chopped

6 small zucchini (courgettes)

120 ml (4 fl oz) olive oil

2 cloves garlic, finely diced

1 brown onion, finely diced

4–6 ripe tomatoes, grated

salt, to taste

freshly ground black pepper

1 lemon

parsley for serving

Method

Prepare the amaranth leaves by washing well under cold water and chop roughly. Slice the zucchini into small discs.

In a large pot heat the olive oil and sauté the onions until soft, add the garlic and grated tomato, combine well and allow to simmer on a low heat for 4–5 minutes. Add the sliced zucchini and continue cooking for a further 5 minutes. Add the amaranth leaves and combine gently. You can add a little water if it looks too dry, 120 ml (4 fl oz) should be enough.

Simmer for 10–12 minutes or until the vegetables are tender. Shake the pot a little instead of mixing to keep vegetables whole.

Season to taste. Sprinkle with parsley and a squeeze of lemon before serving.

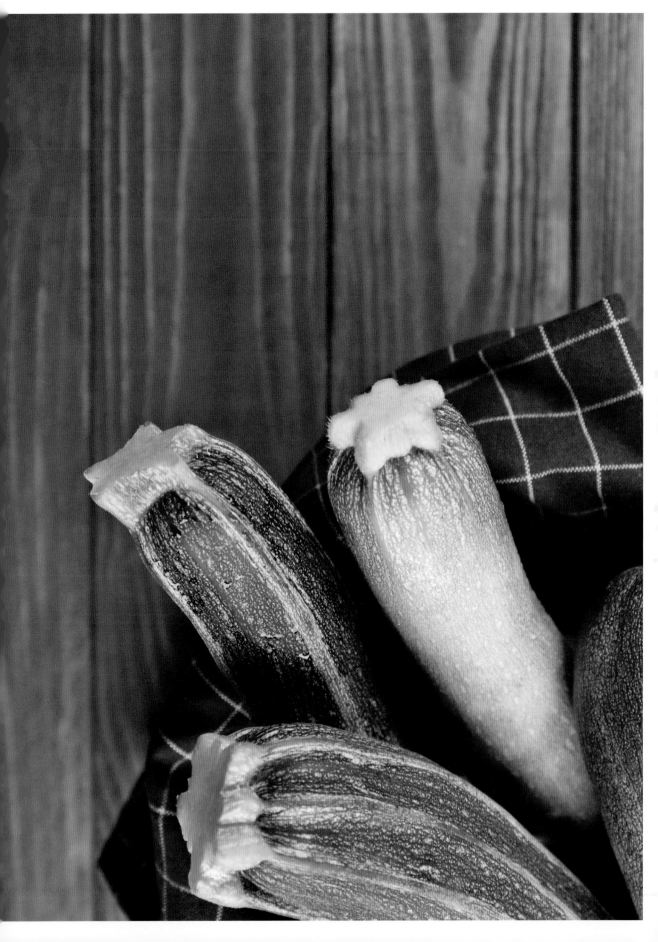

Lemon and Oregano Potatoes

Serves 6

Ingredients

2 kg (4 lb) potatoes

juice of one lemon

80ml (2 2/3 fl oz) olive oil

salt and pepper

oregano

Method

Preheat oven to 200°C (400°F).

Wash and peel potatoes.

Cut into quarters and combine with lemon juice, olive oil, salt, pepper and oregano. Transfer into a baking dish and bake for about 45 minutes or until cooked (depending on the size of the potatoes). I sometimes add a little water into the baking dish.

Serve with roast meats.

SPANISH OMELETTE

Serves 4

Ingredients

4 large potatoes

80 ml (2 2/3 fl oz) olive oil

2 large onions, peeled and sliced

6 eggs

salt and pepper, to taste

chopped parsley, to garnish

Method

Prepare potatoes by peeling and slicing into thin slices, about 5 mm (1/5 in).

Pour in the olive oil into a deep frying pan heat. Add the potatoes and onions and cook on a medium heat, turning occasionally, until they are cooked. This should only take about 10–12 minutes. Pour out any excess oil from the frying pan.

In a large bowl, beat the eggs using a fork and season.

Pour over the potatoes and onions and cook over a medium heat. When the sides are cooked you can slide it onto a plate and then place the frying pan over the plate and return the omelette to the pan upside down. Return to the heat and cook the other side.

Serve hot or warm.

SOUPS

MINESTRONE

Serves 4 to 6

Ingredients

1 red onion, finely diced

1 clove garlic, finely diced

olive oil

2 carrots, peeled and diced

1 celery stalk, sliced thinly

2 zucchini (courgette), diced

1 potato, peeled and diced

200 g (7 oz) spinach, washed and chopped

20 ml (2/3 fl oz) tomato paste (concentrate)

1 x 400 g (14 oz) can diced tomatoes

1 bay leaf

1/2 teaspoon sugar

100 g (3 1/2 oz) small pasta like ditali

1 x 400 g (14 oz) can borlotti beans

handful of basil leaves

fresh Parmesan, for grating

Method

In a large pot, sauté the onions and garlic in a little olive oil until soft.

Add the vegetables, tomato paste and the can of diced tomatoes and combine.

Add 2 1/2 L (approx. 5 pints) water and bring to the boil. Add the bay leaf and sugar.

Simmer for about 30 minutes. Add the pasta and drained beans and continue cooking for a further 15- 20 minutes. If the soup is starting to look too thick, you can add some more water.

Season with salt and pepper and add the basil. Serve sprinkled with grated Parmesan.

Fisherman's Stew

Serves 4 to 6

Ingredients

1 small whole firm-fleshed fish, cleaned

1 whole garlic clove

6 black peppercorns

salt

1 brown onion, peeled and sliced

olive oil

3 celery stalks, cleaned and sliced

2 cloves garlic, finely diced

3 tomatoes, peeled and chopped

3 potatoes, peeled and chopped into chunks

3 carrots, peeled and sliced

2 bay leaves

500 g (1 lb) fish fillets (I like to use firm fish)

parsley, chopped, to garnish

1 lemon

Method

In a large saucepan, place the whole fish and cover with about 1½ L (52 oz) of water. Add the whole garlic clove and season with salt and add peppercorns. Bring to the boil and simmer for 30 minutes. Drain and remove the garlic, peppercorns and bones, keeping the stock and flesh from the fish. This will serve as the fish stock base for the stew.

In a large pot, sauté the onions in a little olive oil. Add the celery, garlic and tomatoes and cook until soft, this should only take 4 to 5 minutes. Add potatoes and carrots, bay leaves and season well. Add the fish stock (there should be about a liter (36 oz), if not add some water) and simmer gently for 30 minutes. Add the fish fillets and flesh from the stock and simmer for a further 20 minutes. When cooked, remove some of the potatoes from the soup and mash with a fork then add them back to the soup.

Add the parsley and a squeeze of lemon. Serve hot in bowls with fresh crusty bread.

Bean, Vegetable and Chorizo Soup

Serves 4 to 6

Ingredients

400 g (14 oz) dried white beans (butter or cannellini)

1 onion, finely diced

1 clove garlic, finely diced

olive oil

1 x 400 g (14 oz) can diced tomatoes

20 ml (2/3 fl oz) tomato paste (concentrate)

1 teaspoon sugar

1 bay leaf

2 carrots, peeled and diced

2 zucchini (courgette), diced

2 celery stalks, chopped

1 potato, peeled and diced

1 chorizo, chopped into chunks

1/2 teaspoon smoked paprika (optional)

salt and pepper, to taste

fresh parsley, chopped, to garnish

Method

Soak the beans in cold water overnight.

In a large pot, sauté the onion and garlic in a little olive oil or until soft.

Drain the beans and add to the pot and pour in about 2 liters (approx. 4 pints) of water.

Add the tomatoes, tomato paste, sugar and bay leaf and stir well.

Add the vegetables and bring to the boil. Simmer for 30 minutes, then add the chorizo and paprika. Continue cooking for a further 30 minutes or until the beans are cooked.

Season to taste and add the parsley. Serve hot.

LENTIL SOUP

Serves 4

Ingredients

500 g (1 lb) brown lentils

1 onion, finely diced

2 cloves garlic , finely chopped

olive oil

1 x 400 g (13 oz) cans of diced tomatoes

2 bay leaves

oregano salt and pepper, to taste

20 ml (2/3 fl oz) vinegar

Method

Wash the lentils and drain in a colander. Sauté the onions and garlic in a little olive oil in a large pot. Add drained lentils, tomatoes, bay leaves and oregano. Pour in 1 L (approx. 2 pints) of water and bring to the boil. Simmer until the lentils are cooked.

Season to taste and pour in the vinegar at the end.

Serve hot accompanied with feta cheese, olives, pickled vegetables and fresh bread.

You can also add diced carrots and celery to this soup if desired.

TOMATO AND BASIL SOUP

Serves 4 to 6

Ingredients

1 onion, finely diced

1 clove garlic, finely diced

olive oil

1 kg (approx. 2 lb) ripe tomatoes, peeled, seeded and chopped

4 teaspoons tomato paste (concentrate)

2 teaspoons sugar

salt and pepper, to taste

handful of basil, chopped

Method

In a large pot, sauté the onions and garlic in a little olive oil. Add the chopped tomatoes and combine. Add 1 liter (2 pints) of water, tomato paste and sugar and stir well. Season with the salt and pepper and the basil, reserving a few leaves to sprinkle over the soup before serving.

Simmer for about 30 minutes. Pour into bowls, sprinkle with some of the saved basil leaves and serve immediately with fresh crusty bread.

Avgolemono Soup with Chicken

Serves 4 to 6

Ingredients

750 g (approx 1 1/2 lb) chicken pieces (thighs, legs and wings are good for stock)

160 g (5 1/2 oz) short grain rice

salt, to taste

freshly ground black pepper

egg and lemon sauce (see recipe page 214)

Method

Place the chicken pieces in a large pot of water, about 1 1/2 liters (approx. 3 pints). Bring to boil and simmer until the chicken is cooked and tender. Remove the chicken and strain the stock. You should have about 1 liter (2 pints) of stock.

Bring the stock back to the boil and add the rice. Simmer for about 10–12 minutes or until rice is tender. Turn off the heat. Season to taste.

Add the prepared egg and lemon sauce slowly to the soup. You can shred the cooked chicken and return to the soup or serve it as an accompaniment.

Serve immediately.

AVGOLEMONO SOUP WITH MEATBALLS

Serves 4 to 6

Ingredients

500 g (1 lb) minced beef

1 small onion, finely diced

90 g (3 oz) short/medium grain rice

10 g (1/3 oz) parsley, chopped

4 teaspoons mint or dill, finely chopped

salt and pepper

50 g (1 oz) butter

egg and lemon sauce (see page 214)

Method

In a large bowl, combine mince, onion, half the rice, herbs and seasonings. Shape this mixture into small balls.

Pour 1 1/4 L (approx. 2 1/2 pints) water into a large saucepan and add butter.
Bring to the boil. Slowly add the meatballs into the boiling water, together with the remaining rice.
Cook for approximately 20 minutes, or until cooked.

Make the egg and lemon sauce and add to the soup.

Season to taste, garnish with a sprig of parsley if you wish, and serve hot.

Avgolemono Soup with Fish

Serves 6

Ingredients

1 small onion, peeled and quartered

2 carrots, scrubbed and halved

2 celery stalks, chopped into quarters

2 large potatoes, peeled and cut into chunks

10 peppercorns

salt

1 1/2 kg (3 lb) whole firm fish

olive oil

lemon juice

90 g (3 oz) short/medium grain rice

egg and lemon sauce (see page 214)

salt and pepper, to taste

white pepper, to garnish

Method

Cook vegetables together with peppercorns and salt in a large saucepan of water.

While they are cooking, wash and clean fish. If the fish is large, cut into half and place into the boiling water with the vegetables. Simmer for about 15 minutes or until fish is done.

Remove fish and vegetables carefully with a slotted spoon and put aside. Place vegetables onto a platter. Remove flesh from the fish and arrange onto the platter as well. Drizzle some olive oil and lemon juice.

Sieve stock into a clean pot and bring to the boil. Add rice and simmer until cooked.

Add egg and lemon sauce and season to taste.

Garnish with white pepper. Serve hot accompanied by the fish and vegetables.

This light and healthy soup is lovely with some feta cheese, olives and fresh bread.

PIES, PASTRIES AND BREADS.

Greek-style Pissaladière

Serves 4

Ingredients

olive oil

3 onions, finely sliced

1 pizza base

150 g (5 oz) black olives, pitted and halved

100 g (3 1/2 oz) feta cheese

Method

Preheat oven to 180°C (350°F).

In a frying pan, heat some olive oil and add the finely sliced onions. Simmer until soft and lightly golden.

Place your pizza base on a lightly oiled tray and top with the onion. Place the olives on top and crumble the feta cheese over the onion mix. Place in the oven and bake for about 15 to 20 minutes or until cooked and base is golden around the edges.

LEEK AND GOAT'S CHEESE TART

Serves 4

Ingredients

1 sheet store-bought shortcrust pastry (not sweetened)

3 leeks, trimmed and sliced thinly

olive oil

2 eggs

200 ml (7 fl oz) pouring cream

200 g (7 oz) goat's cheese

salt and pepper, to taste

Method

Preheat the oven to 200°C (400°F).

Roll out the pastry and line a little buttered tart shell. Using a fork, prick the base and cook for 10-12 minutes or until golden. Remove from the oven and leave aside.

In a large frying pan, sauté the leeks in a little olive oil until soft. Add the eggs and cream and season. Stir well to combine and pour into the prepared quiche shell. Dot with pieces of goat's cheese and bake in the oven for about 20-25 minutes or until cooked.

QUICHE LORRAINE

Serves 4 to 6

Ingredients

1 sheet store-bought shortcrust pastry (not sweetened)

200 g (7 oz) thick-sliced bacon, trimmed and diced

4 eggs

120 ml (4 fl oz) crème fraîche

salt and pepper, to taste

Method

Preheat the oven to 200°C (400°F).

Roll out the pastry and line a little buttered tart mould. Using a fork, prick the base and cook for 10-12 minutes or until golden.

Sprinkle the bacon evenly over the quiche base.

In a bowl, lightly whisk the eggs and creme fraiche using a fork. Season to taste and pour mixture over the bacon.

Bake in the oven for about 20 minutes or until set.

Serve hot with a green salad.

OLIVE OIL FLATBREAD

Serves 4 to 6

Ingredients

60 ml (2 fl oz) olive oil

30 g (1 oz) fresh yeast or 7 g (1/4 oz) dry yeast

300 ml (10 fl oz) warm water

4 teaspoons sugar

400 g (13 oz) plain bread flour

1 teaspoon salt

4 teaspons sesame or poppy seeds

oregano or rosemary (optional)

Method

In a medium bowl crumble the fresh yeast or scatter the dry yeast, add the sugar and add the warm water. Mix well, cover with a tea towel and allow to rest for 10 minutes, or until it begins to bubble. Add the flour, salt and olive oil mixing with a wooden spoon until all combined and then continue mixing with your hands until it resembles a soft dough.

Pour the dough out onto a working bench and knead until it is smooth and elastic. You can also use an electric mixer with a dough hook if you prefer.

Put the dough back into a clean bowl and cover with cling wrap and a tea towel. Allow it to sit for about an hour for the yeast to activate and the dough to rise.

Preheat the oven to 200°C (400°F). Roll out the dough on a lightly floured working bench, 1 cm (1/2 in) thickness, and place onto a lightly oiled baking tray. Brush the dough with a little water and sprinkle with the seeds or salt. You may like to sprinkle with some herbs instead. I like oregano or rosemary.

Make indentations with your fingers (if you want) all over the dough. Bake for about 45 minutes or until the dough is cooked through. Remove from the oven, allow to cool a little and serve warm.

Olive Flatbread

Brush the rolled-out dough with olive oil instead of water, and sprinkle with 100 g (3 1/2 oz) halved kalamata olives and 1 teaspoon oregano.

Tomato and Onion Flatbread

Heat the olive oil in a large frying pan and add the onions. Cook for about 5–6 minutes or until soft. Add the tomatoes and continue cooking for a further 5 minutes. Remove from heat and spread the mixture evenly over the prepared dough in the baking dish. Sprinkle with the oregano, thyme, salt and pepper to taste and bake as instructed.

Spanakopita (Spinach Pie)

Serves 4 to 6

Ingredients

200 g (6 1/2 oz) melted butter mixed with 125 ml (4 oz) olive oil

500 g (1 lb) spinach

300 g (10 oz) feta cheese
(if you prefer, you can use ricotta cheese instead of the feta or a combination of both, which is what I like to do)

3 eggs

pinch of nutmeg

125 ml (4 oz) milk

black pepper, to taste

filo pastry (homemade or store-bought)

Method

Preheat oven to 200°C (400°F). Prepare a large baking dish by brushing with a little melted butter and oil. Wash the spinach, drain, dry and chop roughly. Place into a large bowl. Add crumbled feta cheese, eggs, nutmeg and milk. Mix well. Season with black pepper. Place a sheet of the pita filo or 6–8 sheets prepared filo pastry into the prepared baking dish. Pour the spinach mixture over, then cover with more filo.

Score the pastry and brush with butter/oil mixture. Moisten edges together and crimp. Sprinkle with a little water before putting into oven.

Bake for about 30–40 minutes, or until pastry is golden and crispy.

Sprinkle with some more water once you have taken it out of the oven.

Serve immediately. This is delicious with tzatziki.

You can also make individual spanakopitas (pictured) by cutting the filo into strips and placing 1 spoonful of filling at one end, then folding the right corner over to the left to make a triangle. Fold again upwards to make another triangle. Continue until you have a neat triangle parcel. Brush with butter and oil mixture and cook until golden and crispy.

Tiropitakia (Cheese Pie)

Serves 4 to 6

Ingredients

200 g (7 oz) melted butter mixed with 120 ml (4 oz) olive oil

300 g (10 oz) feta or ricotta cheese (whichever you prefer, or a combination of both)

3 eggs

120 ml (4 oz) milk

filo pastry (homemade or store-bought)

Method

Preheat oven to 200°C (400°F).

Prepare a large baking dish by brushing with a little melted butter and oil.
Mix cheese, eggs and milk well.
Place 6–8 sheets prepared filo pastry into the prepared baking dish. Pour the cheese mixture over, then cover with more filo.

Score the pastry and brush with remaining butter/oil mixture. Moisten edges together and crimp. Sprinkle with a little water before putting into oven, this helps to prevent the filo pastry curling up too much.

Bake for about 30–40 minutes, or until pastry is golden and crispy.

Take out of the oven and sprinkle again with a little water.

Serve immediately.

You can make individual tiropitakia (cheese triangles) following the method used to make individual spanakopita.

PIZZA AND PASTA

Pizza Dough

Makes about 3 pizza bases

Ingredients

25 g (3/4 oz) fresh yeast or 1 7 g (1/4 oz) sachet dried yeast

1 teaspoon sugar

handful of bread flour, extra

500 g (1 lb) strong white bread flour 00

20 ml (2/3 fl oz) olive oil

1 teaspoon salt

Method

Place the yeast, together with the sugar and 300 ml (10 fl oz) warm water, in a bowl, add 2 to 3 tablespoons of flour to make a paste and mix well. Cover with a tea towel and allow to rest in a dry, warm spot in your kitchen.

Place the bread flour in another bowl, make a well in the centre and pour in the olive oil. Add the yeast mixture and mix. You can add a little more flour or water at this point if you need to.

Turn the dough out onto your bench or board, flour your hands and knead for about 8–10 minutes. The dough should be smooth and soft. Place into a clean bowl, cover with a tea towel and allow to rest in a warm place for about an hour. It should double in size.

When it has risen, knead it again for a few minutes and then divide into about three balls for medium-sized pizzas or more if you are making small pizzas.

Lightly oil your pizza trays and roll out the dough to size. Place the rolled-out dough onto the tray, ready for the toppings to go on.

TOMATO SAUCE FOR PIZZA TOPPING

Makes about 500 ml (approx. 1 pint)

Ingredients

1 small onion, finely diced

1 clove garlic, finely diced

25 g (3/4 oz) unsalted butter

olive oil

1 kg (2 lb) ripe tomatoes, peeled, seeded and chopped

1 teaspoon sugar

small bunch fresh basil leaves, torn

salt and pepper, to taste

Method

In a large saucepan, sauté the onion and the garlic in the butter and a little olive oil until soft. Add tomatoes, sugar, basil, salt and pepper. Simmer for about 20–25 minutes.

You can, of course, use bottled tomato passata if you prefer. Use this sauce as the base for your pizza, with a variety of delicious toppings.

Pizza Topping Ideas

Vegetables

Grilled capsicum (bell pepper)

Zucchini (courgette)

Pumpkin

Potato (thinly sliced)

Caramelized onion

Mushroom

Olives

Meats

Salami

Prosciutto

Ham

Chorizo

Anchovies

Cheeses

Mozarella

Tallegio (this goes nicely with potato and caramelized onion)

Feta

Parmesan

Herbs and spices

Basil

Oregano

Chili (flakes or powder)

Homemade Pasta

Serves 4 to 6

Ingredients

400 g (14 oz) 00 flour

4 large organic eggs

pinch of salt

20 ml (2/3 fl oz) olive oil

Method

Pour the sifted flour onto a wooden board or your bench top and make a well.

Break the eggs into the well and add a pinch of salt and oil. I like to use my hands but you can use a fork to stir some flour into the eggs. Keep adding more flour until it is all combined. Dust your bench or board with some more flour and knead the dough until it forms a silky ball.

Cover with a kitchen cloth and allow to rest for about 20 minutes.

If you have a pasta machine, you can use that or if not you can simply roll out balls of dough with a rolling pin and cut into shapes or strips.

Cook in a large saucepan of salted water for about 4–5 minutes, ready for your preferred sauce or just some butter.

The flour you should use is 00 flour as it is very fine and higher in gluten, making it easier to use.

LASAGNE

Serves 4 to 6

Ingredients

1 large brown onion, finely diced

olive oil

2 cloves garlic, finely diced

2 carrots, peeled and diced

375 g (13 oz) minced (ground) pork

375 g (13 oz) minced (ground) veal

1 x 680 ml (23 oz) bottle
tomato passata

120 ml (4 fl oz) white wine

4 teaspoons fresh parsley, chopped

4 teaspoons fresh basil, chopped

1 bay leaf

1 teaspoon sugar

salt and pepper to taste

250 g (9 oz) lasagne sheets
(or use homemade pasta sheets)

120 g (4 oz) mozzarella cheese, grated

60 g (2 oz) Parmesan cheese, grated

bechamel sauce (See page 218)

Method

In a large saucepan, sauté the onion in a little olive oil until soft. Add the garlic and carrots and cook a little more. Add the pork and veal mince and brown, stirring well. Add the tomato passata and wine and combine. Add the parsley, basil, bay leaf, sugar and season well. Cover and cook gently for about 30 minutes.

Preheat the oven to 180°C (350°F). To assemble the lasagne, pour about 3 to 4 spoonfuls of the meat sauce into a lasagne dish. Place a layer of lasagne sheets and pour over one-third of the meat sauce. Carefully drizzle one-third of the béchamel sauce over the meat sauce. Sprinkle one-third of the mozzarella and Parmesan over the béchamel. Repeat this order for the second layer.

Place a third layer of lasagne sheets on top and pour over the remaining meat sauce then the remaining béchamel sauce and top with remaining cheese. Bake in the oven for about 45 minutes or until golden brown. Serve hot with a green salad.

Spaghetti Bolognese

Serves 4 to 6

Ingredients

1 onion, grated

1 clove garlic, finely chopped

olive oil

600 g (1 lb 5 oz) minced (ground) beef

1 bottle (680 ml/23 oz) tomato passata

250 ml (8 fl oz) red wine

4 teaspoons oregano

1 bay leaf

1 teaspoon sugar

salt and pepper, to taste

small bunch of fresh basil

400 g (14 oz) spaghetti (or use homemade pasta — see page 104)

15 g (1/2 oz) butter

Parmesan cheese

Method

In a large saucepan, sauté onions and garlic with a little olive oil. Add the mince and brown. Pour in the tomato passata, 360 ml (12 fl oz) water and the red wine and mix well.

Add oregano, bay leaf and sugar and season to taste with the salt and pepper. Pick about eight basil leaves and tear into the sauce. Cook gently for about an hour, keeping an eye on it and stirring occasionally. You can add a little more water if it begins to look too dry.

When sauce is almost ready, prepare your spaghetti. Bring salted water to boil in a large saucepan. Add the spaghetti and follow the cooking instructions on the packet. Drain spaghetti in a colander when ready and then pour back into the pot, add the butter and stir. Divide spaghetti onto plates and, using a ladle, pour over the Bolognese sauce and grate some Parmesan on top. You can sprinkle some fresh basil leaves on top and it's ready to serve.

Spaghetti Carbonara

Serves 4 to 6

Ingredients

400 g (14 oz) spaghetti (or use homemade pasta — see page 104)

olive oil

6 slices bacon or pancetta, sliced

3 large eggs

4 teaspoons fresh parsley, chopped

salt and pepper

100 g (3 1/2 oz) Parmesan cheese, grated

Method

In a large saucepan, bring salted water to a boil and add the pasta. Cook following instructions on the packet. If using fresh pasta, cook for about 4 to 5 minutes.

While pasta is cooking, heat up a little olive oil and fry the diced pancetta for a couple of minutes or until golden. Remove from the frying pan into a bowl and set aside. In another bowl, whisk the eggs, parsley, salt and pepper and half the cheese. Add the pancetta.

When pasta is cooked, drain in a colander and pour straight into the egg mixture and stir well.

Divide on to plates and sprinkle the remaining Parmesan cheese on top and serve immediately.

Calamari with Macoroni

Serves 4 to 6

Ingredients

1 kg (approx. 2 lb) calamari, cleaned and cut into small pieces

105 ml (3 1/2 fl oz) olive oil

1 onion, peeled and diced

1 clove garlic, finely diced

1 bay leaf

120 ml (4 fl oz) red wine

400 g (14 oz) tinned tomatoes

2 heaped tbs parsley, finely chopped

1/2 teaspoon paprika

1/2 teaspoon sugar

salt, to taste

freshly ground black pepper

240 g (8 oz) short macaroni

Method

Sauté the onion in the olive oil in a large pot until soft. Add the prepared calamari, stir and cook for a few minutes or until the calamari changes color. Add the garlic, bay leaf, red wine, tomatoes and paprika, sugar and combine well. Bring to the boil, mix well then lower the heat and simmer for about 30 minutes. You can add some water if necessary, 240 ml (8 fl oz) should be enough.

While the calamari is cooking, cook the macaroni in some water until tender and cooked through. Drain and add to the calamari when it is almost ready. Mix through well and serve with some extra parsley sprinkled over.

PAELLA

Serves 4 to 6

Ingredients

olive oil

1 onion, peeled and diced

2 chorizo, sliced

2–3 roasted red capsicums (bell peppers), sliced (from a jar is fine)

2 cloves garlic, finely diced

pinch of saffron

500 ml (approx. 1 pint) paella rice (I like to use bomba)

1 x 400 g (14 oz) can diced tomatoes

salt and pepper, to taste

120 ml (4 fl oz) white wine

1 L (approx. 2 pints) stock (fish, vegetable or chicken, whatever you prefer)

12 large prawns (shrimp)

150 g (5 oz) squid, cleaned and sliced into small pieces

150 g (5 oz) firm flesh fish, cut into pieces

fresh parsley, for garnish

1 lemon, cut into wedges

Method

In a large paella pan, sauté the onion and sliced chorizo in a little olive oil until soft. Then stir in the red capsicum, garlic, saffron and mix well. Add the rice and diced tomatoes and combine. Pour in the wine and the stock and bring to the boil. Simmer for 10–15 minutes, stirring as it cooks. If it is starting to look too dry, add some more water.

In the meantime, wash and prepare your seafood. Add to the rice mixture when the rice is almost cooked. The seafood should only need about 5 minutes until it is ready to eat. Sprinkle with the parsley, season to taste and serve with lemon wedges.

Stuffed Tomatoes with Calamari, Rice and Herbs

Serves 4 to 6

Ingredients

8 tomatoes

105 ml (3 1/2 fl oz) olive oil

1 small brown onion, finely diced

1 clove garlic, finely diced

210 g (7 oz) risotto rice

500 g (17 1/2 oz) calamari, cut into small pieces

4 teaspoons parsley, finely chopped

60 g (2 oz) pine nuts

Salt, to taste

Freshly ground pepper, to taste

480 ml water

Method

Preheat the oven to 180°C (350°F). Prepare the tomatoes by washing them and slicing the tops off. Carefully scoop out the flesh using a teaspoon. Remove the seeds, chop finely and set aside to use in the filling later.

Heat the olive oil in a pan and sauté the onions until softened. Add the garlic, risotto rice and stir well to coat the rice with the oil. Add the tomato flesh and water and simmer for about 15 minutes or until the rice is tender. Add the diced calamari and cook for a few minutes. Add the pine nuts, herbs and season to taste. Spoon mixture into the prepared tomatoes, put lids on and arrange in a baking dish, drizzle with some olive oil and add 240 ml (8 fl oz) of water into the dish. Bake in the preheated oven for approximately 35 minutes or until cooked.

Serve hot or at room temperature with fresh crusty bread.

Risotto with Asparagus, Peas, Mint and Parmesan

Serves 4 to 6

Ingredients

500 g (1 lb) green asparagus

50 g (1 3/4 oz) unsalted butter

20 ml (2/3 fl oz) olive oil

1 small brown onion, finely diced

500 ml (approx. 1 pint) risotto rice
(I like to use Carnaroli)

240 ml (8 fl oz) sweet or dry white wine

750 ml (approx. 1 1/2 pints) stock
(I like to use chicken stock)

120 g (4 oz) peas
(I usually use frozen peas)

10 g (1/3 oz) mint, chopped

Parmesan cheese, freshly grated, to serve

Method

Prepare the asparagus by trimming the woody ends and washing well. Cut each asparagus stalk into three or four pieces and set aside.

In a large saucepan, add the butter and olive oil. When the butter has melted, add the onion and asparagus and sauté until soft. Add the rice and mix well.

Pour in the wine and keep stirring until most of the wine has been absorbed, then add the stock a ladleful at a time. You may need more water or stock if the rice is not quite cooked. Just before the rice is cooked, stir in the peas and combine well, then sprinkle in the mint and season to taste.

Serve with a generous amount of freshly grated Parmesan.

VEGETABLES
AND
SALADS

STUFFED TOMATOES

Serves 4

Ingredients

8 tomatoes

1 small onion, finely diced

olive oil

250 ml (approx. 1/2 pint) risotto rice

15 g (1/2 oz) parsley, chopped

10 g (1/3 oz) dill, chopped

10 g (1/3 oz) mint, chopped

sea salt

freshly ground black pepper

Method

Prepare your tomatoes by washing them and slicing off the tops. Keep the tops as you will use them later as a lid. Scoop out the flesh using a teaspoon and set aside. Remove the seeds and chop up the flesh.

Sauté the onion in a pan with a little olive oil until soft. Add the rice, tomato flesh, herbs and season to taste. Cook for 5–6 minutes. Spoon mixture into the tomatoes, put tomato lids on and arrange in an ovenproof dish. Drizzle with a little olive oil and pour about 240 ml (8 fl oz) of water into the dish. Bake in a preheated oven for approximately 45 minutes to an hour or until cooked.

Serve hot from the oven with a green salad and some fresh crusty bread.

Eggplant Rolls with Feta, Olives and Sundried Tomato

Serves 4 to 6

Ingredients

60 ml (2 fl oz) olive oil

2 large eggplant (aubergines), trimmed and sliced into 1 1/2 cm (1/2 in) thickness lengthways

60 g (2 oz) feta cheese, crumbled

60 g (2 oz) kalamata olives, pitted and diced

12 sundried tomatoes, diced

small handful of basil leaves

4 teaspoons parsley, fined chopped

salt, to taste

freshly ground black pepper

Method

In a bowl combine the feta, olives, sundried tomatoes, parsley and mint.
Prepare the eggplant and brush the slices with olive oil. Heat a frying pan with a little extra olive oil over a medium heat and fry the eggplant slices, about 2–3 minutes on each side or until cooked. You can also cook the eggplant over a grill or barbeque if you prefer. Allow it to sit on some absorbent paper while cooking the remainder of the eggplant. Season to taste.

Lay out each eggplant slice and place a heaped spoonful of the feta mixture at the wider end and roll up tightly. Place onto a serving platter and drizzle a little more olive oil over, a grind of black pepper and some extra herbs.

My Insalata Caprese

Serves 4

Ingredients

4 ripe tomatoes, chopped into chunks

4 rounds buffalo mozzarella

red wine vinaigrette (see page 213)

large handful basil leaves

salt and pepper, to taste

Method

Onto a large platter, place the chopped tomatoes.
Tear the mozzarella balls into pieces and scatter amongst the tomatoes.
Pour the dressing over the tomato and mozzarella and sprinkle with the basil leaves.
I like to combine all the ingredients with my hands gently and serve.

Lentil, Beetroot and Goat's Cheese Salad

Serves 4

Ingredients

3 medium-sized beetroot

150 g (5 oz) lentils

1 leek, trimmed and sliced

olive oil

200 g (7 oz) goat's cheese

60 g (2 oz) walnuts, chopped

honey and orange dressing
(see page 213)

salt and pepper, to taste

Method

Place the beetroot in a saucepan of water and bring to the boil. Simmer for about 20 minutes or until the beetroot is tender. Remove from the water and gently rub off the skin and cut into chunks. Set aside.

If you are using lentils from a can, drain and set aside in a bowl. If using dried lentils, wash and pick through dried lentils carefully before cooking. You will need to boil the lentils in a large saucepan of water for about 30–40 minutes or until cooked. Drain and put aside.

In a frying pan sauté the leeks in a little olive oil until soft.

To assemble, simply place the lentils into a large salad bowl,
top with the beetroot and sautéed leeks. Pour the dressing over the salad and combine gently. Crumble the goat's cheese over the salad and sprinkle the walnuts on top.

Serve immediately.

MY NIÇOISE SALAD

Serves 4

Ingredients

4 tomatoes, cut into wedges

1 baby cos (romaine) lettuce, outer leaves removed

1 small red onion, sliced

2 potatoes, cooked and sliced

200 g (7 oz) green beans, steamed or lightly boiled

4 hard-boiled eggs

150 g (5 oz) black olives

1 x 185 g (6 oz) can good-quality tuna in oil

4 marinated anchovies, sliced

red wine vinaigrette (see page 213)

Method

Place all the prepared vegetables, eggs and olives into a large salad bowl. Drain the tuna, break it up and scatter it and the anchovies onto the salad.

Pour dressing over the salad.

Combine gently I like to use my hands to do this and serve.

Watermelon and Haloumi Salad

Serves 4 to 6

Ingredients

30 ml (1 fl oz) olive oil

1 kg (2 lb) watermelon, cut into chunks

240 g (8 oz) haloumi cheese, sliced to 1 cm (1/2 in) thickness

1/2 Spanish onion, finely sliced (optional)

10 g (1/3 oz) fresh mint leaves

15 g (1/2 oz) parsley, finely chopped

1 lemon

Method

Fry or grill the haloumi on a medium/high heat for 2–3 minutes on each side until golden brown. Place the watermelon chunks into a large serving bowl, drizzle with the olive oil, and a good squeeze of lemon and add the herbs and onion (if using). Add the haloumi and using your hands combine gently.

Variations

Watermelon, haloumi with shrimp: add 24 cooked shrimp to the salad and combine gently.

Watermelon, haloumi with chicken: add 120 g (4 oz) shredded cooked chicken and one handful baby spinach to salad and combine gently.

Greek Salad with Purslane

Serves 4 to 6

Ingredients

3 tomatoes cut into wedges

1 red onion, peeled and sliced

1 cucumber, sliced

1 green pepper (capsicum), sliced

1 handful of purslane (you can use rocket instead if you cannot get a hold of purslane)

10 g (1/3 oz) chopped dill

10 g (1/3 oz) chopped parsley

10 g (1/3 oz) chopped mint

4 teaspoons dried oregano

100 g (3 1/2 oz) kalamata olives

salt, to taste

60 ml (2 fl oz) olive oil

20 ml (2/3 fl oz) red wine vinegar

120 g (4 oz) feta cheese, cubed or crumbled

Method

Arrange the tomatoes, onions, cucumber, pepper, purslane and herbs in a serving bowl. Mix gently and top with olives and feta cheese.

Pour the olive oil, vinegar, oregano and seasonings into a jar, close the lid and shake until all the ingredients are blended.

Drizzle over the salad and serve.

Bulgur Wheat Salad

Serves 4 to 6

Ingredients

30 ml (1 fl oz) olive oil

1 small red onion, finely diced

200 g (7 oz) bulgur wheat

500 ml (approx. 1 pint) water

salt, to taste

freshly ground black pepper, to taste

seeds of one pomegranate

100 g (3 1/2 oz) raisins or currants

15 g (1/2 oz) fresh mint, finely chopped

15 g (1/2 oz) fresh parsley, finely chopped

60 g (2 oz) pumpkin seeds

rind of one orange

lemon

Method

Place the bulgur wheat in a bowl and pour over enough boiling water to cover. Cover the bowl and leave for about 20 minutes.

Put the bulgur wheat in a serving dish and add the onion, pomegranate seeds, herbs, pumpkin seeds and orange rind. Combine gently and drizzle with olive oil and squeeze half a lemon over. Season to taste.

ROASTED VEGETABLE SALAD WITH BULGHUR

Serves 4

Ingredients

1 red onion, peeled and cut into wedges

2 cloves garlic, finely diced

1 sweet potato, peeled and cut into chunks

2 zucchini (courgette), sliced thickly

2 red capsicum (bell pepper), seeded and cut into chunks

olive oil

150 g (5 oz) bulghur

100 g (3½ oz) baby spinach

red wine vinegar

oregano, to taste

salt and pepper, to taste

75 g (2½ oz) pumpkin seeds

Method

Preheat the oven to 180°C (350°F).

Place all the prepared vegetables in a large baking tray and drizzle with olive oil.
Mix to combine and bake in an oven for about 45 minutes or until vegetables are cooked but not too soft.

In the meantime, bring to boil some water in a large saucepan and add the bulghur, simmer for about 20 minutes. Drain in a colander and allow to cool.

Place the baby spinach onto a platter, place the vegetables on the spinach and then the bulghur. Dress with some vinegar, sprinkle with oregano and season to taste. Gently combine all the ingredients. I like to do this with my hands.

Scatter the pumpkin seeds over and serve.

GREEN BEANS AND TOMATO SALAD

Serves 4 to 6

Ingredients

400 g (14 oz) green beans

4 large ripe tomatoes, chopped

1 teaspoon dried oregano

1 red onion, peeled and sliced

15 g (1/2 oz) parsley, finely chopped

15 g (1/2 oz) mint, finely chopped

15 g (1/2 oz) dill, finely chopped

salt, to taste

fresh ground black pepper, to taste

chunks of day old bread (optional)

feta, to serve

olives, to serve

120 ml (4 fl oz) olive oil

60 ml (2 fl oz) red wine vinegar

Method

Place the beans into a pot of salted boiling water for about 2–3 minutes. Drain and place the beans in a pot of cold water to stop the cooking process and keep the color. Drain well and dry on some paper toweling.

Transfer the beans to a serving dish and add the tomatoes, onion, herbs and season to taste. Combine gently and drizzle over the olive oil and red wine vinegar. Add the bread (optional) and using your hands gently combine all the ingredients.

Perfect on its own with fresh crusty bread, feta and olives or with any meat, fish or poultry.

Spinach Salad with Fresh Figs and Goat's cheese

Serves 4 to 6

Ingredients

150 g (5 oz_ baby spinach leaves

45 ml (1 1/2 fl oz) olive oil

20 ml (2/3 fl oz) balsamic or red wine vinegar

60 g (2 oz) pumpkin seeds

100 g (3 1/2 oz) soft goat's cheese

60 g (2 oz) sultanas

6 fresh ripe figs, quartered

salt, to taste

freshly ground black pepper

Method

In a large bowl pour in the olive oil and vinegar and mix well. Place the spinach leaves in the dressing and combine using your hands gently.

Take the leaves out of the dressing and place onto a serving dish. Place the quartered figs onto the spinach and sprinkle with crumbled goat's cheese, sultanas and pumpkin seeds.

Drizzle a little more olive oil over and season to taste.

Village-style Eggplant Salad

Serves 4 to 6

Ingredients

2 medium-sized eggplants (aubergines)

olive oil

salt and freshly ground black pepper, to taste

salad greens (I like to use both rocket and cos as I love them together)

4 tomatoes, cut into wedges

I red onion, sliced

basic balsamic vinaigrette (see page 213)

I roasted red capsicum (bell pepper), cut into strips

100 g (3 1/2 oz) feta cheese

Method

Trim eggplants and cut into cubes. Heat a little olive oil in a large frypan and fry the cubed eggplant in batches. Drain on kitchen paper. Allow the eggplant to cool and season with a little salt and pepper.

Place salad greens, tomatoes and onions in a large salad bowl and toss with the dressing.

Add the cooked eggplant, red capsicum and crumble the feta cheese on top. Serve with crusty fresh bread.

Perfect for a simple summer lunch.

ROCKET AND ORANGE SALAD

Serves 4

Ingredients

2 teaspoons honey

1 teaspoon mustard

45 ml (1 1/2 fl oz) vinegar

100 ml (3 1/2 oz) extra virgin olive oil

2 teaspoons orange juice

2 teaspoons sesame seeds

500 g (1 lb) rocket leaves

500 g (1 lb) salad leaves

2 oranges

250 g (8 oz) Greek Graveria or Kasseri cheese

Method

To make the dressing, whisk the honey, mustard, vinegar, olive oil, orange juice and sesame seeds until combined.

Wash rocket and salad leaves and place onto a large salad platter. Remove the peel from the oranges and slice thinly into rounds, carefully removing any bitter pith. Slice the cheese thinly into bite-sized pieces. Arrange cheese and orange slices onto the greens and pour over the dressing.

Delicious served with keftethes and fresh crusty bread or as part of a meze meal.

TOMATO, ROASTED RED PEPPER AND CHORIZO SALAD

Serves 4

Ingredients

1 chorizo

olive oil, for frying

4 tomatoes or a punnet of cherry tomatoes

2 roasted red peppers (store-bought is fine), sliced

1 small red onion, sliced

100 ml (3 1/2 oz) extra virgin olive oil

45 ml (1 1/2 oz) red wine vinegar

pinch of ground cinnamon

salt and pepper, to taste

15 g (1/2 oz) fresh parsley, chopped

piece of feta (optional)

Method

Slice and gently fry the chorizo in a little olive oil.

In a large salad bowl, add the tomatoes, peppers and red onion. Prepare the dressing by whisking the olive oil and vinegar together. Pour over the salad, sprinkle the cinnamon and season to taste.

Add the chorizo and sprinkle with the parsley. Combine all the ingredients gently using your hands.

Serve with fresh crusty bread. I like a little feta cheese with my salad also and be sure to mop up all the dressing with your bread.

Beetroot and Yoghurt Salad

Serves 4

Ingredients

3–4 medium-sized beetroot

120 ml (4 fl oz) Greek yoghurt

20 ml (2/3 fl oz) olive oil

20 ml (2/3 fl oz) balsamic vinegar

fresh mint leaves, chopped, to taste

1 clove garlic, finely diced

salt and pepper, to taste

30 g (1 oz) raw, unsalted and shelled pistachios

Method

Trim the beetroot and place in a large saucepan of water and bring to the boil. Simmer for about 20-30 minutes or until cooked. Remove from the water and gently rub off the skin. Cut into chunks or slices, whatever you prefer, and place into a bowl.

In another bowl, add the yoghurt, olive oil, vinegar, mint leaves and garlic and season. Mix gently and pour over the beetroot. Combine and scatter with nuts.

WILD GREENS SALAD WITH POMEGRANATE

Serves 4

Ingredients

400 g (14 oz) salad greens
(spinach, endive, radicchio, chicory,
chard, arugula (rocket))

210 g (7 oz) pomegranate seeds

60 ml (2 fl oz) olive oil

4 teaspoons honey

1 teaspoon pomegranate molasses

30 ml (1 fl oz) red wine vinegar

1 fennel bulb, finely sliced

1 orange, remove the skin and pith and
cut into segments,

salt, to taste

freshly ground pepper

45 g (1 1/2 oz) toasted pine nuts

Method

Arrange the salad greens onto a serving platter. Add the fennel and orange segments.

Place the olive oil, vinegar, honey, pomegranate molasses and seasonings into a jar, cover tightly and shake until all the ingredients are blended.

Sprinkle pomegranate seeds and pine nuts over and drizzle with the dressing to serve.

OLIVE OIL ROASTED VEGETABLES

Serves 4 to 6

Ingredients

150 ml (5 fl oz) olive oil

2 eggplants (aubergines)

3 zucchini (courgette)

2 carrots

6 potatoes

2 red onions

1 green capsicum (bell pepper)

1 red capsicum (bell pepper)

4 tomatoes, grated

15 g (1/2 oz) chopped parsley

salt, to taste

freshly ground black pepper

4 teaspoons dried oregano

Method

Preheat the oven at 180°C (350°F). Cut the eggplant into chunks, sprinkle with salt and allow it to sit in a colander for 30 minutes. Rinse and dry well.

Place all the prepared vegetables into a large baking dish and pour over the olive oil. Add the parsley, oregano, season with salt and pepper and combine gently. Add 120 ml (4 fl oz) water and cover with foil. Bake for about 2 hours.

Remove foil and bake for a further 30 minutes or until vegetables are cooked through and golden.

Braised Cauliflower with Tomato and Smoked Sweet Paprika

Serves 4 to 6

Ingredients

1 small brown onion, diced

olive oil

1 medium cauliflower, cut into florets

2 large ripe tomatoes, grated

1 teaspoon smoked sweet paprika

salt and pepper, to taste

flat-leafed parsley, freshly chopped, to garnish

Method

Sauté onion in a large pan with a little olive oil. Add cauliflower and brown a little.

Put the grated tomato on the cauliflower and add enough water to cover. Add the smoked sweet paprika and season to taste. You can add more or less paprika, depending on how much heat you like ... I always like to add a little more.

Cover and cook until cauliflower is just tender. Garnish with parsley.

Serve alone with some fresh crusty bread or as a side to fish or meat dishes.

I prefer to shake the pan from side to side when I check the cauliflower during the cooking process, rather than stirring, so I don't break the florets.

STUFFED EGGPLANT (PAPOUTSAKIA)

Serves 4 to 6

Ingredients

4 eggplant (aubergines)

olive oil

1 small brown onion, finely diced

1 clove garlic, finely diced

500 g (1 lb) minced (ground) beef

3 large tomatoes, peeled, seeded and chopped

salt and pepper, to taste

1 teaspoon sugar

small handful parsley

1/4 teaspoon cinnamon

1/4 teaspoon nutmeg

1/2 portion béchamel sauce (see page 218)

kefalotiri cheese, for grating

Method

Slice eggplant lengthways into halves. Sprinkle the cut side with some salt and let sit for about 30 minutes in a colander, cut side down, to drain away the bitterness.

Heat some olive oil in a large frying pan and fry the eggplant for about 2-3 minutes per side. Remove from pan and allow to cool. Scoop the flesh from the eggplant, being careful not to tear the skin. Chop the flesh and place in a bowl. Lay the hollowed-out eggplant into a baking dish. Sauté the onion in oil until soft. Add the garlic, minced beef, chopped tomatoes, salt and pepper, sugar, parsley and spices. Simmer for about 5 minutes then add the eggplant flesh and combine well. Fill the hollowed-out eggplant with the meat mixture. Make the béchamel sauce. Melt the butter in a saucepan and stir in the flour until combined. Pour in the warm milk slowly, whisking constantly. Add the egg and nutmeg and season to taste. Stir until thick. Spoon the sauce over the meat, smoothing it out. Grate some cheese on top. Pour about 240 ml (8 fl oz) of water in the dish and bake in the oven at 180°C (350°F) for about 45 minutes or until cooked.

SEAFOOD

GRILLED OCTOPUS

Serves 4 to 6

Ingredients

1 (approx. 1 kg/32 oz) medium octopus, cleaned

salt, to taste

freshly ground black pepper, to taste

olive oil

dried oregano

lemon wedges

Method

Place the cleaned octopus into a large pot of water, enough to cover completely. Simmer on a low heat for about 1 hour. Remove carefully, drain and pat dry.

Place on a hot grill or barbeque, turning over as it turns a golden color. You may prefer to cut the octopus into pieces before cooking or cut it after it has been cooked.

Arrange onto a platter and drizzle some olive oil over, sprinkle with dried oregano, season to taste with salt and freshly ground black pepper and lemon wedges.

Serve hot.

Grilled Calamari

Serves 4 to 6

Ingredients

750 g (1 1/2 lb) calamari rings

oil and lemon dressing (see Dressings and Sauces)

oregano

Method

Cook the calamari rings over a hot grill or barbeque quickly, turning as soon as you see the edges charring: a couple of minutes will do.

Place onto a platter and pour over the dressing and oregano. Serve immediately.

Great as a meze or, together with a salad and some fresh crusty bread, this makes a delicious light lunch.

Grilled Sardines

Serves 4 to 6

Ingredients

12 sardines, cleaned

100 ml (3 1/2 fl oz) olive oil, for brushing and serving

15 g (1/2 oz) parsley, finely chopped

2 garlic cloves, finely diced

4 teaspoons capers

2 lemons, cut into wedges

zest of one lemon

salt, to taste

freshly ground black pepper

Method

To make the marinade, in a large bowl use half the olive oil and add the parsley, garlic, lemon zest and capers.

Heat the grill and lightly brush with some olive oil. Place the sardines on the hot grill and brush with the marinade. Turn over after 2 or 3 minutes and brush again, cook for a further 2 to 3 minutes or until cooked.

Serve on a platter with lemon wedges and season to taste with the salt and pepper.

CALAMARI STIFADO WITH RISONI

Serves 4 to 6

Ingredients

1 kg (approx. 2 lb) calamari, cleaned and cut into pieces

105 ml (3 1/2 fl oz) olive oil

105 ml (3 1/2 fl oz) white wine

12 small (pearl) onions, peeled and left whole

2 bay leaves

10 cloves

zest of one orange

pinch of cinnamon

4 large ripe tomatoes, grated

salt, to taste

ground black pepper, to taste

250 g (8 1/2 oz) risoni

4 teaspoons dill, finely chopped

zest of 1/2 orange

Method

In a large casserole pot, heat the olive oil and sauté the onions for a couple of minutes. Add the calamari, wine, bay leaves, cloves, orange zest, cinnamon, grated tomatoes and 240 ml (8 fl oz) of water. Season to taste. Simmer for 30 minutes or until the calamari is cooked.

In the meantime cook the risoni in water until tender. Drain the risoni and add to the cooked calamari and mix through.

Serve scattered with a little extra dill and orange zest.

Salt Cod, Potato and Tomato Bake

Serves 4 to 6

Ingredients

500 g (1 lb) salt cod

1 large onion, peeled and finely sliced

olive oil

6 potatoes, peeled and sliced into rounds

4 tomatoes, grated

salt and pepper, to taste

1 tablespoon oregano

1 heaped tablespoon parsley, chopped

Method

Soak the salt cod in cold water overnight.

Preheat the oven to 180 C (350 F). In a large baking dish, sauce the onion in a little olive oil. Place the potatoes in the dish, together with the grated tomato.

Season with salt and pepper, add oregano and parsley and combine.

Remove the salt cod from the water and cut into individual portions.

Add the potato mixture and mix well. Pour a little water into the dish, drizzle with olive oil and bake in the oven for about 1 hour or until cooked.

Serve with a green salad.

SHRIMP AND SCALLOPS WITH CHERRY TOMATOES AND PEPPERS

Serves 4 to 6

Ingredients

300 g (10 oz) shrimp (prawns), peeled and deveined

300 g (10 oz) scallops, cleaned and halved

60 ml (2 fl oz) olive oil

1 teaspoon sugar

1 red capsicum (pepper), diced

1 green capsicum (pepper), diced

500 g (approx. 1 lb) cherry tomatoes, halved

105 ml (3 1/2 fl oz) white wine

4 teaspoons dried oregano

2 cloves of garlic, finely diced

4 spring onions (scallions), thinly sliced

parsley, finely chopped, to garnish

1 lemon, to serve

salt, to taste

freshly ground black pepper

Method

In a large frying pan heat the olive oil and sauté the scallions and garlic until soft. Add the pepper, tomato, oregano, sugar and wine. Mix well and simmer for 10–15 minutes. If it is getting too dry add 120 ml (4 fl oz) of water. Add the shrimp and scallops, mix gently and continue cooking for another few minutes until the shrimp and scallops are cooked.

Season to taste. Serve with a drizzle of olive oil, a squeeze of lemon and a sprinkling of feta cheese and parsley.

STUFFED CALAMARI

Serves 4

Ingredients

4 calamari (cleaned)

olive oil

1 small onion, finely diced

375g (12 1/2 oz) long-grain rice

1 tomato, peeled, seeded and diced

splash of white wine

salt and pepper, to taste

1 teaspoon parsley, finely chopped

pinch of chili (optional)

Method

Ask your fishmonger to clean the calamari for you as it saves a lot of time. To prepare the calamari, cut the tentacles off and chop them into small pieces.

In a large frying pan, heat a little olive oil and sauté the tentacles and onion. Add the rice, tomato and splash of white wine. Simmer for about 6–8 minutes. You may need to add a little water if it is looking too dry. Season with the salt and pepper and add the parsley. You can add some chili if you like a little heat.

Using a spoon, fill the calamari bodies with the rice mixture three-quarters full, as the rice will swell as it cooks. Secure the opening with a wooden toothpick.

Place the stuffed calamari into a baking dish and add about 240 ml (8 fl oz) of water and a drizzle of olive oil. If you have any rice left, you can put that in the baking dish with the filled calamari. Cover and bake in the oven for 30 minutes or until cooked.

FRIED FISH

Serves 4

Ingredients

100 ml (3 1/2 fl oz) olive oil

1 kg (32 oz) whole firm fish, cleaned

150 g (5 oz) plain flour

salt, to taste

freshly ground black pepper

lemons for serving

Method

Wash and pat dry the fish.

Place the plain flour on a plate and press the fish onto the flour until all sides are covered. Shake off any excess flour.

In a large frying pan heat the olive oil. Add the fish and cook on each side for about 6–7 minutes, or until golden and cooked through.

Season with salt and pepper and serve with lemon slices.

Salmon Poached in Olive Oil

Serves 4 to 6

Ingredients

4–6 pieces of salmon

1 L (approx. 2 pints) olive oil

salt, to taste

freshly ground black pepper, to taste

fresh parsley, chopped roughly

Method

Place salmon in a large deep frying pan and pour over the olive oil until it covers the salmon. Poach on a low heat for approximately 20–30 minutes or until salmon is cooked. Carefully remove salmon from the oil and drain on some paper toweling.

Season with salt, freshly ground black pepper and sprinkle with parsley. Serve with potato or green salad.

Salmon with Lentil Salad

Serves 4 to 6

Ingredients

210 g (7 oz) green lentils

8 mushrooms, sliced thinly

1 carrot, grated

1 red onion, finely sliced

2 tomatoes, cut into chunks

6 slices smoked salmon or a piece of salmon poached in olive oil torn into chunks

90 ml (3 fl oz) olive oil

45 ml (1 1/2 fl oz) red wine vinegar

salt, to taste

freshly ground black pepper

fresh parsley and dill for serving

Method

Rinse the lentils under cold water and pour into a large saucepan with plenty of water to cover the lentils. Bring to the boil and simmer for about 15 minutes or until the lentils are cooked but still al dente, remove from the heat and allow to cool.

Place the cooked lentils in a serving bowl and add the mushrooms, carrot, onion, tomatoes and combine gently.

Pour the olive oil, vinegar and seasonings into a jar, close tightly and shake until blended. Drizzle over the salad and combine gently.

Top with the poached salmon (or smoked salmon) and an extra drizzle of olive oil and scattered with herbs for serving.

FISH EN PAPILLOTE

Serves 4

Ingredients

4 whole white firm fish, approximately 450 g (15 oz) each

75 g (2 1/2 oz) pitted green olives, diced

60 ml (2 fl oz) olive oil

1 small fennel, sliced finely keeping the fronds

4 tomatoes, sliced

15 g (1/2 oz) parsley, finely chopped

10 g (1/3 oz) dill, finely chopped

salt, to taste

freshly ground black pepper

4 pieces of greaseproof paper, large enough to hold the fish

Method

Preheat the oven at 200°C (400°F). Clean the fish well and dry with paper towels.
In a frying pan heat half the olive oil and sauté the sliced fennel for about 5–6 minutes or until soft. Season to taste.

Prepare the paper by cutting out squares large enough to hold the fish with enough room to fold over the edges to seal all the ingredients.

Fold paper in half, open up and place a quarter of the sautéed fennel in the centre on one side of the crease. Place one fish on the fennel and top with olives, sliced tomatoes, chopped parsley and dill.

Bring the other side of the paper over the fish. Beginning at one end of the opening fold over 1 cm (1/2 in) of the edge. Keep folding all the way around the opening until it resembles a semicircle parcel. Repeat this to make the seal even tighter.

Place the parcels onto a baking tray and bake for about 20–25 minutes. Serve on a large plate, slit open the parcel with a knife.

BAKED FISH

Serves 4 to 6

Ingredients

4 large onions, sliced

2 cloves garlic, finely chopped

olive oil

6 fresh tomatoes, chopped

250 g (8 oz) finely chopped parsley

salt and pepper, to taste

1 1/2 kg (3 lb) fish (I like to use a firm fish)

lemon slices

Method

Preheat oven to 200°C (400°F).

Sauté the onions and garlic in a large baking dish with a little olive oil. Add chopped tomatoes, parsley and season to taste. Add 120 ml (4 oz) water and combine well. Place the cleaned fish on the mixture and cover with some of the sauce. Bake for 30–40 minutes, or until fish is cooked.

Serve hot with potatoes and a green salad.

MEAT AND POULTRY

Souvlaki

Serves 6

Ingredients

1 1/2 kg (3 lb) shoulder lamb, cut into bite-sized cubes

375 ml (12 oz) olive oil, divided

2 lemons

5 cloves garlic, diced

8 teaspoons oregano

240 ml (8 oz) red wine

salt and pepper, to taste

12 flat breads

tzatziki

1/2 shredded iceberg lettuce

6 tomatoes, sliced

tomato sauce (optional)

Method

Place meat into a bowl and pour in 120 ml (4 fl oz) of olive oil, juice of 1 lemon, diced garlic, oregano and red wine. Mix well and allow to marinate in the refrigerator for at least a few hours, ideally overnight.

When ready to grill or barbecue the souvlaki, drain the meat, reserving the marinade, and thread onto skewers. Add the remaining olive oil, juice of another lemon and seasonings to the marinade and mix well. Use this to baste the souvlaki while they cook.

Rest the cooked souvlaki on a plate while grilling flat breads. Brush the bread with a little marinade and cook them lightly until golden and warm.

Place the meat from the skewers onto the bread, together with some tzatziki, lettuce and tomatoes.

Add tomato sauce if desired. Roll up and enjoy.

BRAISED CHICKEN WITH CINNAMON

Serves 4 to 6

Ingredients

6 chicken thighs
(on the bone and skin on)

100 ml (3 1/2 fl oz) olive oil

2 large ripe tomatoes
(peeled, seeded and diced)

4 onions, quartered

1 cinnamon stick

20 black peppercorns

60 g (2 oz) currants

salt, to taste

Method

In a large heavy saucepan heat the olive oil. Add the chicken and cook on a medium heat for 6–8 minutes or until lightly golden. Take the chicken out using a slotted spoon and place onto a platter. Add the onions to the saucepan and cook until softened, about 5–6 minutes. Return the chicken to the saucepan adding the tomatoes, cinnamon stick, peppercorns and currants. Add about 120-240 ml (4-8 fl oz) of water and season to taste.

Cover and simmer for 40 minutes or until the chicken is cooked. Serve with rice, pasta or potatoes. Serve hot.

SHOULDER OF LAMB SLOW ROASTED

Serves 4 to 6

Ingredients

2–2 1/2 kg (approx. 4-5 lb) lamb shoulder

105 ml (3 1/2 fl oz) olive oil

8 teaspoons dried oregano

4 garlic cloves, crushed, skins left on

salt, to taste

freshly ground black pepper

240 ml (8 fl oz) water

4 lemons (2 for juicing and 2 for serving)

4 potatoes, cut into large chunks (optional)

Method

Preheat the oven to 180°C(350°F). Place the shoulder of lamb in a baking dish, drizzle with the olive oil, squeeze over the juice of the 2 lemons, and sprinkle the oregano and season with salt and pepper.

Cover with foil and bake for approximately 1 1/2 hours. Reduce the heat to 150°C (300°F) and continue cooking for a further 2 hours. You can add the potatoes at this point if you are using them. Remove the foil, mix potatoes gently and cook in the oven for another 20–30 minutes at 180°C (350°F) or until golden and cooked.

Season the potatoes and serve the lamb with extra lemon wedges.

ONE POT CHICKEN WITH RISONI AND SPINACH

Serves 4 to 6

Ingredients

4–6 chicken thighs

60 ml (2 fl oz) olive oil

240 ml (8 fl oz) tomato passata

1 small bunch of spinach, chopped

salt to taste

freshly ground black pepper

parsley, finely chopped, to garnish

500 g (approx. 1 lb) risoni

Method

In a large saucepan brown the chicken in the olive oil. Add the tomato passata and 480 ml (16 fl oz) of water. Bring to the boil, and simmer for 10 minutes. Add the risoni and spinach and simmer for a further 15 minutes or until the chicken and risoni are cooked.

You can add a little more water if it is looking too dry.

Season well and sprinkle with the parsley. Serve with feta cheese.

MEATBALLS WITH CUMIN IN TOMATO

Serves 4

Ingredients

80 ml (2 2/3 fl oz) olive oil

500 g (approx. 1 lb) minced beef or veal

2 thick slices day old bread, crusts removed

120 ml (4 fl oz) milk

1 onion, finely chopped

1 egg

15 g (1/2 oz) parsley, finely chopped

1/2 teaspoon ground cumin

salt, to taste

freshly ground black pepper

plain flour for coating

2 x 400 g (14 oz) can diced tomatoes

1/2 teaspoon sugar

1 teaspoon oregano

20 ml (2/3 fl oz) red wine vinegar

1 clove garlic, finely diced

Method

Place the bread in a bowl and cover with the milk. Leave until the milk has been soaked up. In a large bowl place the mince, onion, egg, parsley, cumin and the bread (squeeze out any excess milk before adding). Season to taste and mix well with your hands or a wooden spoon. Take about a walnut size of mixture in your hands and mould into an oval shape.

In a frying pan heat half the oil and add the garlic and sauté for 1–2 minutes. Add the tomatoes, sugar, oregano and vinegar. Season to taste and simmer for 10–12 minutes.

In another frying pan pour the remaining oil and add the meatballs. Cook until golden, turning over so they are browned all over. Add the tomato sauce over and bring to the boil. Turn the heat down and simmer for a further 15–20 minutes. Shake the frying pan a little to make sure all the sauce is evenly distributed.

Pastitso

Serves 4 to 6

Ingredients

750 g (1 1/2 lb) rigatoni

15 g (1/2 oz) butter

salt

1 onion, finely chopped or grated

1 clove garlic, finely chopped

olive oil

700 g (1 1/2 lb) minced beef

1 x 680 ml (22 oz) bottle tomato passata

splash of red wine

salt and pepper, to taste

1 bay leaf

1 teaspoon oregano

100 g (3 1/2 oz) feta cheese

béchamel sauce (see page 218)

Method

Preheat oven to 200°C (400°F).

Cook pasta in a large pot of water. When cooked, drain and toss in the butter and season with a little salt.

Sauté onions and garlic in a large saucepan with a little olive oil. Add the mince and brown. Add the tomato passata and 300 ml (10 fl oz) water. Mix well and add a splash of red wine. Season to taste. Add oregano and bay leaf. Cook for about 20 minutes, or until almost cooked.

While the pasta and meat sauce are cooking, prepare the béchamel sauce and set aside.

In a large baking dish, place half the pasta, then top with mince mixture and crumble the feta cheese over. Top with the remaining pasta and then the béchamel sauce. Bake for 45 minutes or until golden brown.

Serve with a delicious big Greek salad.

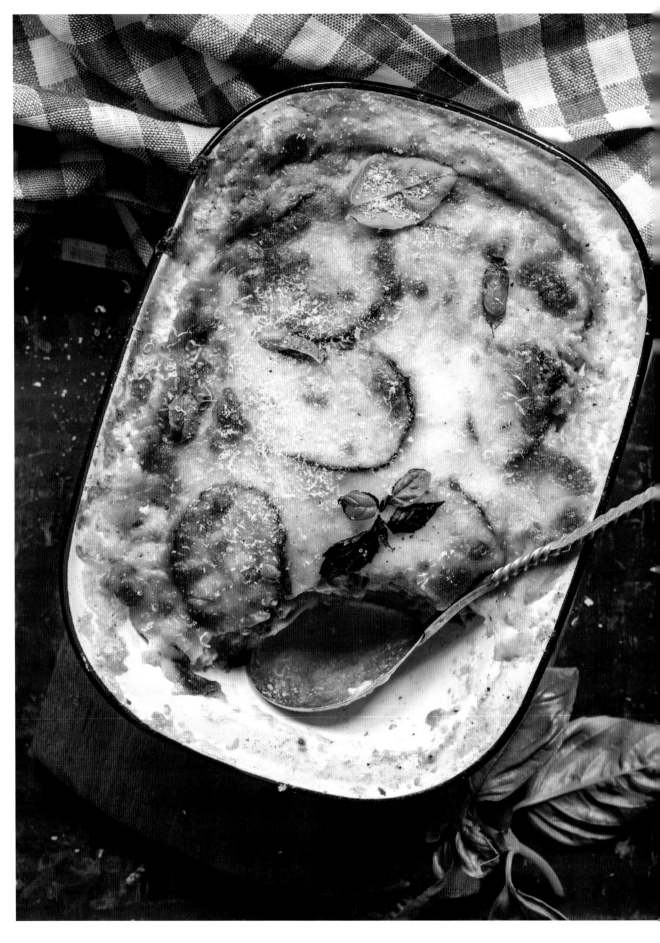

MOUSSAKA

Serves 4 to 6

Ingredients

4 large eggplants (aubergines), sliced

salt

4 large potatoes, peeled and sliced

olive oil

1 large onion, finely diced or grated

2 cloves garlic, finely diced

750 g (1 1/2 lb) minced beef

1 x 680 ml (22 oz) bottle tomato passata

1 bay leaf

1 teaspoon oregano

salt and pepper, to taste

béchamel sauce (see page 218)

100 g (3 1/2 oz) feta cheese

Method

Preheat oven to 200°C (400°F). Wash and trim eggplant. Slice, sprinkle with salt and leave to drain for half an hour. Rinse and pat dry with paper towels. Peel and slice potatoes and leave in a bowl of water so they don't brown.

Heat a little olive oil in a frying pan and fry the potatoes until golden brown. Place them onto some kitchen paper to absorb any excess oil when cooked. Fry the eggplant, using the same frypan with any remaining oil. They may need a little more attention as they will tend to absorb more oil than the potatoes.

In a heavy saucepan, heat oil and sauté onions and garlic until soft. Add beef and stir until brown. Add tomato passata, 250 ml (8 fl oz) of water, bay leaf, oregano and season to taste.

Pour a little olive oil into a baking dish and arrange eggplant slices. Top with a layer of potatoes. Pour the meat mixture on top and crumble over the feta cheese. Arrange the remaining eggplant and potatoes. Pour prepared béchamel sauce on top of the vegetables and bake for about 45 minutes, or until golden.

PORK WITH LEEKS

Serves 4 to 6

Ingredients

3–4 bunches leeks

olive oil

1 small onion, finely diced or grated

11/2 kg (3 lb) pork shoulder or leg, cut into chunks

500 ml (17 oz) tomato passata

salt and pepper

1 teaspoon sweet paprika (optional)

ground black pepper, to taste

Method

Wash and trim leeks well and cut into 4 cm (1 1/2 in) pieces, set aside.

Heat oil in a large casserole dish and sauté onions and meat until brown. Add tomato passata and season to taste. Pour in 500 ml (16 oz) of water, cover and cook until pork is almost done. Add the leeks and continue simmering until the meat and leeks are tender. Add more water if it looks too dry.

Serve hot and garnish with ground pepper. Serve with feta cheese and fresh crusty bread.

Greek Roast Pork

Serve 4 to 6

Ingredients

1 1/2 kg (3 lb) leg of pork

salt and pepper, to taste

4 teaspoons dried rosemary

juice of 1 lemon

juice of 1 orange

5 garlic cloves, halved

Method

Preheat oven to 200°C (400°F).

Prepare the meat by washing and patting dry with some kitchen paper. Using a sharp knife, score the top into square or diamond shapes.

Place the pork onto a roasting pan and, using your hands, rub salt, pepper, rosemary, lemon and orange juice all over the meat. Tuck the garlic into the skin where you have scored it.

Place into oven and cook for about 1 1/2 hours. I always like to pour a little water into the baking dish as well, about 250 ml (1/2 pint) is fine. The meat won't need turning but baste it with the juices in the pan occasionally, adding more water if you think it is getting too dry.

Turn the oven to 220°C (420°F) for the last 20 minutes so that the pork crisps up to a glorious golden brown.

Serve hot with roast potatoes and salad.

CASSOULET

Serves 4 to 6

Ingredients

240 g (8 oz) bacon, diced

1 brown onion, finely diced

45 ml (1 1/2 fl oz) olive oil or duck fat

2 cloves garlic, finely diced

3 carrots, diced

2 stalks celery, sliced

4 teaspoons fresh thyme, finely chopped

4 teaspoons plain (all-purpose) flour

1 L (approx. 2 pints) stock
(I like to use chicken stock)

100 ml (3 1/2 oz) white wine

60 ml (2 fl oz) tomato paste

750 g (11/2 lb) cannellini or haricot beans, soaked overnight in cold water

5 toulouse sausages

5 confit duck legs

bread crumbs, for topping

fresh parsley, finely chopped, to serve

salt and freshly ground black pepper

Method

Preheat the oven to 180°C (350°F). Brown the bacon and onion in a large ovenproof dish in a little olive oil or the duck fat until soft. Add the garlic and stir.

Add the carrot, celery, thyme and flour, mixing well. Pour in the stock and wine together with the tomato paste and the beans. Season well and bring to a simmer for a few minutes.

Cover and cook in the oven for about 1 hour. Take the casserole out of the oven and add the sausage and duck legs. Sprinkle with some breadcrumbs and return to the oven for a further half hour, uncovered.

Serve with a sprinkling of chopped parsley and some fresh crusty bread.

PORK AND CELERY AVGOLEMONO

Serves 6 to 8

Ingredients

olive oil

1 small onion, finely chopped or grated

1 1/2 kg (3 lb) pork shoulder, cut into pieces (if you prefer you can use pork cutlets)

salt and pepper to taste

1 large bunch celery

egg and lemon sauce (see page 214)

ground black pepper

Method

Heat oil in a large casserole dish and sauté onion and meat until slightly brown.

Pour in 500 ml (16 oz) of water, season and cover. Simmer for about 1/2 hour or until meat is tender.

While meat is cooking, wash and trim celery and cut into 4 cm (1 1/2 in) pieces. Add to the meat and cook until celery is soft; do not overcook.

Prepare the egg and lemon sauce and pour into the casserole. Allow to rest for 5–10 minutes, then serve with some ground black pepper.

BEEF STIFADO

Serves 4 to 6

Ingredients

2 kg (4 lb) pickling onions

olive oil

1 kg (2 lb) stewing beef or veal, cut into chunks

1 x 680 ml (22 oz) bottle tomato passata

60 ml (2 oz) red wine

salt, to taste

3 bay leaves

10 peppercorns

6 whole cloves

1/2 teaspoon cinammon

2 cloves garlic, finely chopped

Method

Peel and cut off the tops and tails of the onions and put aside.

In a large casserole dish, heat some olive oil and brown the meat. Add the onions. Pour in the tomato passata and 500 ml (16 oz) water and wine. Season with salt, add bay leaves, cloves, cinammon, garlic and peppercorns.

Cover and simmer for about 1–1 1/2 hours or until meat and onions are tender and soft.

Serve hot.

SAUCES, DRESSINGS AND DIPS

Basic Balsamic Vinaigrette

Ingredients

120 ml (4 fl oz) extra virgin olive oil

60 ml (2 fl oz) balsamic vinegar

salt and freshly ground black pepper, to taste

Method:

Mix oil and vinegar well, and season to taste.

Note: Ingredients can be combined in a jar and shaken. Any extra can be stored in the jar in the fridge and used later.

Variations

Red wine vinaigrette: Replace vinegar with 45 ml (1 1/2 fl oz) red wine vinegar.

Honey and orange dressing: Replace vinegar with red wine vinegar and add 20 ml (2/3 fl oz) Greek honey and 40 ml (1 1/3 fl oz) orange juice.

Pomegranate dressing: Use white wine vinegar and add 20 ml (2/3 fl oz) pomegranate syrup and 20 ml (2/3 fl oz) honey.

Egg and Lemon Sauce (Avgolemono)

Ingredients:

2 eggs, separated

juice of 1 lemon

chicken stock, or pan juices from whatever the sauce will be added to

Method

Lightly whisk the egg white in a bowl, slowly adding the yolks and whisking a little more. Add the lemon juice gradually.

Slowly add in some of the stock or pan juices, from whatever dish you will be adding the egg and lemon sauce to, beating all the time until completely combined.

OIL AND LEMON DRESSING

Ingredients:

100 ml (3 1/2 oz) good-quality extra virgin olive oil

juice of one lemon

1/4 teaspoon salt

1 teaspoon oregano

Method

Whisk the olive oil, lemon juice and salt well, it should look a little creamy. You can use a blender for this if you prefer. Add the oregano and pour into a jar.

Store it in the cupboard or fridge for at least a month. Shake the jar before serving, to combine the dressing again.

Béchamel Sauce

Ingredients

80 g (2 2/3 oz) unsalted butter

1 L (2 pint) full fat milk, warm

2 eggs

120 g (4 oz) plain flour

salt, to taste

freshly ground white pepper

pinch of grated nutmeg

Method

In a saucepan melt the butter and stir in the flour until combined. Pour the warm milk in slowly, stirring all the time as you pour, add the eggs and mix well. Add the nutmeg and season to taste.

Stir and cook until it is a custard consistency.

TZATZIKI WITH DILL

Serves 4 to 6

Ingredients

500 ml (17 fl oz) plain yogurt

60 ml (2 fl oz) olive oil

1 cucumber, peeled, seeded and finely chopped

3 cloves of garlic, finely diced

salt, to taste

dill, finely chopped, to taste

Method

Line a colander with some muslin and pour the yogurt into it. Allow it to drain for 4–6 hours in the refrigerator.

Place the strained yogurt into a bowl and add the olive oil, cucumber, garlic and dill. Season to taste and serve with an extra drizzle of olive oil.

SKORDALIA

Serves 4 to 6

Ingredients

500 g (1 lb) potatoes

3 cloves garlic, crushed

150 ml (5 fl oz) olive oil

juice of one lemon

45 ml (1 1/2 fl oz) white wine vinegar

salt and pepper, to taste

Method

Cook potatoes in plenty of salted water. When cooked, drain and peel while hot.

Using a mortar and pestle or food processor, mash potatoes until you have a puree. Add garlic, then olive oil, lemon and vinegar in turns, beating continuously. You can add a little hot water if it gets too thick.

Variations

Skordalia with walnuts: add 75 g (2 1/2 oz) finely chopped walnuts and two egg yolks to skordalia and combine well.

Butter bean skordalia: reduce olive oil to 60 ml (2 fl oz), replace potatoes with 500 g (1 lb) butter beans (canned is fine).

Fava Dip

Serves 4 to 6

Ingredients

500 g (17 1/2 oz) split yellow peas (fava)

30 ml (1 fl oz) olive oil

1 small onion, grated

salt, to taste

freshly ground black pepper

small handful parsley, finely chopped

Method

Wash the split peas under some cold water in a colander. Add the peas into a large pot of boiling water, about 1 L (approx. 2 pints) and simmer covered for about 30 minutes.

While this is cooking, sauté in a frying pan the grated onion in the olive oil until soft. Add to the split peas and mix well. Add salt to taste. Simmer for another 30 minutes or until the peas have absorbed all the water.

Remove from heat and either blitz with a hand-held blender or stir rapidly with a wooden spoon until smooth.

Spoon onto a serving dish and drizzle some olive oil, a squeeze of lemon and sprinkle with parsley and a grinding of black pepper.

Spicy Feta Dip (Tirokafteri)

Serves 4 to 6

Ingredients

240 g (8 oz) feta cheese

120 ml (4 fl oz) Greek yogurt

20 ml (2/3 fl oz) olive oil

1 teaspoon red wine vinegar

1 roasted red pepper, seeded and minced (can be store bought)

chilli flakes (optional)

Method

In a large bowl, mash the feta cheese together with the yogurt using a fork. Add the olive oil and vinegar and mix well. Add the roasted red pepper and chilli flakes if you want more heat, and combine.

Cover and leave in the refrigerator for at least one hour before serving.

Taramasalata

Serves 4 to 6

Ingredients

6 slices day old white bread
(crusts removed)

240 g (8 oz) salted fish roe

30 g (1 oz) onion, finely diced

240 ml (8 fl oz) olive oil

60 ml (2 fl oz) lemon juice

Method

Soak the bread in a little water, squeeze out excess and crumble.

Using a mortar and pestle, pound the fish roe into a paste. Add the onion, a few drops of oil and keep beating. Add a small amount of bread, along with the oil and lemon juice. Continue adding bread, a little at a time, beating continuously until all is combined. Adding these ingredients slowly will prevent curdling and give you a thick pale pink dip.

Serve with fresh crusty bread.

Note: You can use a food processor if you don't have a mortar and pestle.
Add ingredients slowly.

Two cooked, medium-sized potatoes can be used instead of, or in combination with, the bread.

MELITZANOSALATA (EGGPLANT DIP)

Serves 4 to 6

Ingredients

1 kg (2 lb) eggplant (aubergine)

pinch of salt

3 cloves garlic, crushed

125 ml (4 oz) olive oil

60 ml (2 oz) white wine vinegar (you can use lemon juice if you prefer)

15 g (1/2 oz) parsley, chopped

Method

Preheat oven to 220°C (400°F).

Bake the eggplants for about 40 minutes or until tender.

Run under cold water and peel immediately while still hot. Chop the eggplants and season with salt and garlic.

Use a mortar and pestle, or simply a fork, to mash and combine.

Add the oil, a little at a time, alternating with the vinegar until all used. Fold in parsley and place into a serving dish. Cover and place in the fridge to chill.

Serve with fresh crusty bread.

PICKLES AND PRESERVES

SALT CURED OLIVES

Olives are the simplest of meze dishes, perfect with fresh crusty bread, this for me is typically Mediterranean. I like to use ripe black olives for salt curing and this method gives the olives a wrinkled appearance. You can preserve as many or as little olives as you desire.

Place black olives onto some cheesecloth and cover with a layer of coarse rock salt and suspend over a bucket or place into a colander over a bucket. Toss the olives with the salt daily and the juice will begin to drain.

This process should take about two weeks and you will notice that the olives will begin to look wrinkled. You can check if they are ready by tasting to see if the bitterness has gone and the flesh should be dark all the way through.

When they are ready, rinse them well and you can use them straight away in casseroles or salads.

To store your olives simply pour into sterilized jars filled with salty brine and topped with a little olive oil to seal or only olive oil.

Olives can be stored in a cool dark pantry for up to a year in a sealed jar either in the brine or oil.

PICKLED CABBAGE

Ingredients

1 cabbage

1/2 stick celery

2 L (64 oz) white vinegar

240 g (8 oz) sugar

240 ml (8 oz) olive oil

120 g (4 oz) sea salt

Method

Wash and chop up cabbage roughly into bite-sized pieces. Slice celery finely and add to the cabbage. Place the vegetables into a large bowl.

Place in 2 L (64 oz) water, vinegar, sugar, olive oil and salt into a large saucepan. Bring to the boil and simmer for a couple of minutes. Pour this liquid onto the cabbage and celery mixture, cover and allow it to marinate overnight.

The next day, transfer the pickled cabbage together with some of the liquid into jars or, alternatvely, leave it in a large bowl. Will keep for a couple of weeks in the refrigerator.

Preserving Roasted Red Peppers

Ingredients

8 red capsicums (bell peppers)

DRESSING

100 ml (3 1/2 oz) olive oil

50 ml (1 2/3 oz) red wine vinegar

4 teaspoons fresh parsley, finely chopped

8 basil leaves, torn into pieces

salt, to taste

2 cloves garlic, finely diced

Method

Place the capsicum on a tray into a hot oven at 200°C (400°F) and roast until the skin has blistered and turned almost black, but not burnt.

Remove from the oven and allow to cool. Remove the skin and the seeds and slice into thick strips.

Place into plastic bags, remove as much air as possible and freeze. The capsicum will keep for at least six months.

Thaw when needed and dress with a drizzle of olive oil, vinegar, sprinkled with parsley, basil, garlic and seasoned well with salt.

PICKLED VEGETABLES

Ingredients

1/4 cauliflower

1 green capsicum (bell pepper)

2 red capsicums (bell peppers)

3 stalks celery

3 carrots

2 bay leaves

2 whole garlic cloves, peeled

BRINE

140 g (5 oz) sea salt

210 g (7 oz) sugar

2 L (70 fl oz) white vinegar

240 ml (8 fl oz) olive oil

Method

Prepare the vegetables by cutting the cauliflower into florets. Cut the capsicum into strips and remove seeds. Trim the celery and cut into small pieces. Peel and slice the carrots.

In a large saucepan, bring to boil 2 liters (approx. 4 pints) water, salt, sugar and vinegar and simmer for 4–5 minutes.

Pour this brine over the prepared vegetables in a large bowl and allow to cool.

Transfer the vegetables into two sterilized jars, which will hold 1 L (36 oz) each, and pour over with the brine. Place a bay leaf and a clove of garlic into each jar and seal. The vegetables will keep for 2–3 months. However, once opened, store in the refrigerator.

DESSERT AND SWEET THINGS

DIPLES

Serves 4 to 6

Ingredients

20 ml (2/3 fl oz) olive oil plus oil for frying

3 eggs

250 g (8 1/2 oz) plain flour

1/2 teaspoon baking powder

1/2 teaspoon vanilla paste

2 teaspoon cinnamon, for dusting

120 g (4 oz) walnuts, finely chopped for sprinkling

4 teaspoons finely grated orange rind

SYRUP

240 ml (8 fl oz) honey

240 ml (8 fl oz) water

4 teaspoons sugar

20 ml (2/3 fl oz) lemon juice

Method

In a large bowl whisk the egg whites until fluffy, add the yolks and continue beating for another minute. Slowly begin adding in the flour and mix, add the baking powder and orange rind. Add the vanilla and olive oil, kneading well until dough is soft, elastic and not sticky. Place the dough in a floured bowl and cover with a tea towel, leave for 40 minutes in a warm room.

Sprinkle some flour onto your work surface and divide the dough into two. Roll out each ball of dough as thinly as you can. Cut strips approx 12.5–15 cm x 7.5–10 cm (5-6 in x 3-4 in). Lay strips onto tea towels covered with extra tea towels to avoid drying up.

In a large frying pan pour oil at about 2.5 cm (1 in) deep on a medium-high heat. Using a fork pick up a strip of dough between the prongs and wrap it around the fork. Dip the fork into the boiling oil and swirl it around as the dough wraps around the fork. Remove the fork carefully and fry until golden brown. Remove with a slotted spoon draining any excess oil. Place onto a tray lined with absorbent paper.

Repeat until all dough has been cooked checking the oil is not getting too hot.

Place the ingredients for the syrup into a saucepan, bring to the boil, skim off any froth and remove from the heat. Drop in the diples, one or two at a time and allow to stand for a minute, turning once, then transfer to a serving dish. Have the cinnamon and walnuts in a bowl combined and sprinkle over the diples once they have been placed onto a serving platter.

Continue dipping into the honey and sprinkling with the cinnamon and walnut mixture until all finished. Delicious with a cup of Greek coffee.

Loukoumades (Honey Doughnuts)

Serves 4 to 8

Ingredients

24 g (4/5 oz) dry yeast

750 g (24 oz) plain flour

4 teaspoons sugar

1 teaspoon salt

240 ml (8 fl oz) warm milk

olive oil

honey (warmed)

cinnamon

Method

Sift all the dry ingredients into a large mixing bowl, add 250 ml (8 oz) warm water and the milk and mix into a smooth batter.

Cover and let rest until it has doubled in size, approximately 1 1/2 hours. Make sure the dough is in a warm place.

In a large pot, place enough oil for frying. Take small handfuls of dough and slowly drop them into the hot oil. Cook until golden brown.

Place onto serving dish. Drizzle with warm honey and sprinkle with plenty of ground cinnamon.

Serve immediately.

Bougatsa with Ricotta and Sultanas

Serves 4 to 6

Ingredients

500 g (approx. 1 lb) ricotta cheese

150 g (5 oz) sultanas

2 eggs

50 g (1 2/3 oz) caster (superfine) sugar

1/2 teaspoon ground cinnamon

zest of 1 orange

100 ml (3 1/2 fl oz) olive oil

1 quantity filo pastry (you can make your own or store bought)

Method

Preheat oven to 180°C (350°F). In a large bowl whisk the eggs and sugar until thick and creamy. Add the ricotta cheese and cinnamon and keep whisking. You can use an electric mixer if you prefer. When the mixture is light and fluffy, gently mix in the sultanas and orange zest and put aside.

Have your filo pastry on your work surface covered with a tea towel to prevent drying up. Place a sheet on your bench and brush with a little olive oil then place another sheet on top.

Place 45-60 ml of the ricotta mixture at the bottom third of the filo sheet, leaving a border on either side. Fold in the sides then fold the lower third up. Continue brushing with olive oil as you work. Finally fold the top third down, brush with the olive oil. You should have a rectangle parcel now.

Place onto a baking tray that has been brushed with olive oil and continue making parcels until all the mixture is finished. Sprinkle with a little water before you place in the oven.

Bake for about 15–20 minutes or until golden and crispy. Serve at room temperature.

Fanouropita (St Fanourio's Cake)

Serves 6 to 8

St. Fanourio is the patron saint of lost things. Fanouropita is a cake made in honor of St. Fanourio on the Saints Day when it is made and taken to church for a blessing. This cake is also made many other times of the year, when searching for things that are lost such as jewelry or loves or when searching for an answer.

Ingredients

180 ml (6 fl oz) olive oil

350 g (12 oz) plain (all purpose) flour

4 teaspoons baking powder

1 teaspoon ground cinnamon

150 g (5 oz) caster (superfine) sugar

180 ml (6 fl oz) orange juice

1 teaspoon vanilla extract

60 g (2 oz) raisins

60 g (2 oz) walnuts, chopped

Method

Preheat the oven at 180°C (350°F). Lightly oil a 24 cm (9 1/2 in) cake tin.

Place the flour, baking powder and cinnamon in a large mixing bowl and combine.

Pour in the olive oil, orange juice and vanilla extract and using an electric mixer or a whisk mix well until all combined. Add the raisins and walnuts and mix gently.

Pour into the prepared cake tin and cook in the preheated oven for about 45 minutes or until the skewer that you insert comes out clean. Allow to cool a little before cutting.

You can dust it with a little icing sugar before serving if you like.

Chocolate Tart

Serves 6 to 8

Ingredients

PASTRY

20 ml (2/3 fl oz) olive oil

75 ml (2 1/2 fl oz) water

15 g (1/2 oz) sugar

pinch of salt

90 g (3 oz) unsalted butter

15 g (1/2 oz) almond meal

120 g (4 oz) plain flour

FILLING

250 g (9 oz) pure cream

200 g (7 oz) good-quality milk or dark chocolate (broken into pieces)

1 egg

Method

Preheat the oven to 200°C (400°C).

Place the oil, water, sugar, salt and butter into a heatproof bowl. Place into the oven for approximately 10-12 minutes until the butter has melted and the mixture starts to boil.

Take out of the oven carefully and pour in the almond meal and flour a bit at a time, mixing constantly, until it has formed a ball of dough.

Place the dough on a board and knead it very lightly so it is all combined for a minute and then pat it into a 22 cm (8 1/2 in) round tart tin evenly. Using a fork, dot the base and place in the oven for about 12-14 minute or until it is golden and cooked.

Prepare your filling by simply heating the cream in a saucepan, over a low heat, and adding the chocolate pieces. Stir until the chocolate has melted. Turn the heat off and add the egg, stirring continuously. The mixture should start to look silky.

Pour into your prepared tart mold and bake in the oven for 15-20 minutes. Delicious with some fresh cream and berries.

Oven-Roasted Figs with Ricotta and Honey

Serves 4 to 6

Ingredients

1 kg (approx. 2 lb) fresh figs

50 g (1 2/3 oz) unsalted butter

240 g (8 oz) fresh ricotta

Greek honey

1 teaspoon ground cinnamon

pistachios or crushed walnuts

Method

Prepare the figs by trimming the stems and cutting a cross into the figs but not all the way across the bottom. In a baking dish, melt the butter and place the figs cut side up. Roast for about 10–15 minutes.

Remove from the tray and place onto a platter. Place a heaped spoonful of ricotta into the top of the figs where you have cut. Drizzle with honey and sprinkle with some cinnamon and pistachios or crushed walnuts, whichever you prefer.

Serve immediately.

TARTE TATIN

Serves 4 to 6

Ingredients

6 tart cooking apples

80 g (2 2/3 oz) unsalted butter

120 g (4 oz) caster (super fine) sugar

1 cinammon stick

80 g (2 2/3 oz) sultanas (golden raisins) (optional)

1 sheet store-bought puff pastry

Method

Preheat the oven to 180°C (350°F).

To prepare the apples, peel and cut into quarters and core. Cut the quarters in half again.

In a baking dish, melt the butter and add the sugar. Stir to combine and simmer for 1–2 minutes.

Add the apples and cinnamon stick and cook for a further 2–3 minutes. Add the sultanas now, if using them, and remove the cinnamon stick.

Place the pastry over the apples and tuck into the sides. Bake in the oven for about 20 minutes or until pastry is golden and cooked.

Allow to cool for a couple of minutes before turning out onto a serving dish.

CRÊPES

Serves 4 to 6

Ingredients

260 g (8 1/2 oz) plain (all-purpose) flour

3 eggs

500 ml (approx. 1 pint) warm full-fat milk

30 g (1 oz) unsalted butter, melted

4 teaspoons caster (super fine) sugar

Method

In a large mixing bowl, sift in the flour. Make a well and add the eggs and beat well using a fork. Add the warm milk, melted butter and sugar and keep mixing.

Using a crêpe pan or an oiled frying pan, pour in a ladleful of the crêpe mixture when hot. When the sides of the crêpe look golden and cooked, turn the crêpe over and cook the other side until golden. Continue until all the mixture is finished.

Serve each crêpe with a sprinkling of sugar and a squeeze of lemon or, as my family prefer, smothered with chocolate hazelnut spread.

Stack crêpes on a warm plate or serve each one immediately.

Revani (Semolina Cake with Syrup)

Serves 6 to 8

Ingredients

500 ml (17 fl oz) oil

250 g (8 1/2 oz) caster sugar

6 eggs

juice of 1 orange

1 teaspoon vanilla

250 g (8 1/2 oz) semolina

500 g (17 oz) self-raising flour

250 g (8 1/2 oz) sugar

lemon zest

Method

Preheat oven to 200°C (400°F).

Using an electric mixer, combine the oil and sugar.

Slowly add eggs, one at a time. Add the orange juice, vanilla, semolina and flour and keep mixing until well combined.

Pour into a prepared baking dish and bake for about 30–40 minutes, or until cooked. Allow to cool.

To prepare the syrup, bring 500 ml (17 oz) water, sugar and lemon zest to the boil and simmer for 10 minutes. Pour onto the cake slowly. Once the syrup has been absorbed you can cut into pieces.

Serve at room temperature or cold.

Kourabiedes (Biscuits in Icing Sugar)

Serves 6 to 8

Ingredients

250 g (8 oz) unsalted butter

120 g (4 oz) caster sugar

3 egg yolks

120 ml (4 fl oz) oil

30 ml (1 fl oz) ouzo

1 small teaspoon baking powder

520-650 g (17-21 oz) plain flour

75 g (2 1/2 oz) slivered almonds (optional)

pure icing sugar

Method

Preheat oven to 200°C (400°F).

Cream the butter and sugar until light and fluffy. Add egg yolks and mix well. Pour in the oil, ouzo and baking powder.

Slowly fold in the flour a bit at a time. You may not need all the flour; the dough needs to be light and not sticky. Do not overwork the dough as this can make the kourabiedes tough.

Take a small handful of dough and shape into crescents. Place them onto a baking tray.

Place the slivered almonds in a clean frying pan and toast them over a low heat on the stove top until slighty golden. Sprinkle over the dough.

Bake for about 20 minutes, or until golden brown. Remove from the oven and, using a spatula, transfer onto greaseproof paper. When they are cool, dust with plenty of icing sugar and transfer onto a platter.

These biscuits keep well for about 3–4 weeks.

Halva

Serves 8 to 10

Ingredients

625 g (20 oz) caster sugar

1 cinnamon stick

lemon peel (1/4 lemon)

6–8 whole cloves

240 ml (8 oz) vegetable oil

500 g (17 oz) semolina

120 g (4 oz) chopped almonds (optional)

ground cinnamon, to serve

Method

Put sugar and 1 L (32 oz) water in a large saucepan and stir until sugar is dissolved. Add cinnamon stick, lemon peel and cloves, cover and boil for about 5–7 minutes.

In a large pan, heat the oil, add semolina and brown a little, stirring continuously. Add almonds if desired.

Remove spices from the syrup and slowly start adding to the semolina mixture. Stir until all the syrup is absorbed and the semolina is puffed and soft. It should fall off the spoon cleanly.

Remove from heat and allow to stand for about 10 minutes, then transfer into a large mold or individual smaller ones. Let the molds rest on your kitchen table. When the halva feels firm and has set, unmold and sprinkle with ground cinnamon to garnish.

Serve warm or cold.

KATAIFI NUT ROLLS IN SYRUP

Makes about 20 pieces

Ingredients

1 packet kataifi pastry (available in continental delis)

FILLING

120 g (4 oz) walnuts, chopped

60 g (2 oz) pistachios. chopped

60 g (2 oz) almonds, chopped

1 teaspoon ground cinnamon

120-240 g (4-8 oz) unsalted butter, melted

SYRUP

630 g (21 oz) caster (superfine) sugar

120 ml (4 fl oz) cup honey

6 cloves

1 cinnamon stick

1 tablespoon lemon rind

Method

Combine the nuts and cinnamon in a bowl and set aside.

Take the kataifi pastry out of the packet and spread out onto your bench. Divide into strips about 90 cm (3 ft) long. Place a heaped spoonful of the nut mixture at the top end and roll all the way down to make a roll. Repeat this until all the nut mixture has been used.

Place onto a lightly greased baking tray, in rows, and brush or drizzle with the melted butter. Cover with the foil and bake in an oven at 180 C (350 F) for 30 minutes. Remove the foil and bake for a further 15-20 minutes or until golden. Remove from the oven allow to cool while making the syrup.

In a large saucepan, bring to boil 500 ml (1 pint) of water, the sugar, honey, spices and rind. Simmer for about 8 minutes. Gently pour the hot syrup on the cooled rolls and when all the syrup has been absorbed you can place them onto a platter.

The kataifi will keep well, covered, in the refrigerator for up to a week.

KARYDOPITA
(WALNUT CAKE WITH SYRUP)

Serves 6 to 8

Ingredients

70 g (2 1/3 oz) unsalted butter

150 g (5 oz) caster sugar

3 eggs, separated

70 g (2 1/3 oz) self-raising flour

70 g (2 1/3 oz) semolina

1 teaspoon cinnamon

150 g (5 oz) walnuts, finely chopped

120 ml (4 oz) full-fat milk

240 g (8 oz) caster sugar

lemon zest

4 cloves

Method

Preheat oven to 200°C (400°F).

Cream butter and sugar in a large mixing bowl, add egg yolks and combine. Add flour, semolina and cinnamon and mix well. Add walnuts and milk. Whisk egg whites until light and fluffy and fold into mixture.

Pour into a lightly buttered baking dish and bake for about 45 minutes, or until cooked.

Pour 500 ml (17 oz) water, sugar, lemon zest and cloves in a small saucepan. Simmer for about 10 minutes. Pour over the cake carefully. Leave for about an hour, then cut into pieces. Serve at room temperature or cold.

Galaktoboureko
(Custard Pie with Syrup)

Serves 8 to 10

Ingredients

5 eggs

240 g (8 oz) caster sugar

500 g (17 oz) semolina

1 teaspoon vanilla

3 L (96 fl oz) full-fat milk (warm)

200 g (6 2/3 oz) packet filo pastry

80 ml (2 2/3 fl oz) melted butter

375 g (12 1/2 oz) caster sugar

lemon peel

Method

Preheat oven to 200°C (400°F).

Beat the eggs and sugar until light and creamy. Add the semolina and vanilla and mix well. Pour the mixture into a large saucepan and slowly pour in the warm milk, stirring continuously over a low heat. Keep mixing until mixture is a smooth thick custard. Remove from heat.

In a large baking dish, place half the filo sheets, brushing with the melted butter as you go. Pour in the custard and spread evenly. Continue with the remaining filo sheets. Brush the top layer with melted butter and sprinkle with a little water.

Bake for about 30 minutes or until golden brown. Remove from oven and allow to cool.

To prepare the syrup, bring 500 ml (17 oz) water, sugar and a little lemon peel to the boil and simmer for about 10 minutes. Carefully pour this over the galaktoboureko. When all the syrup has been absorbed and the galaktoboureko has cooled down, cut into pieces. Serve warm or cold.

Rizogalo Rice Pudding

Serves 4 to 6

Ingredients

150 g (5 oz) medium grain rice

600 ml (20 fl oz) full-fat milk

30 g (1 oz) cornflour

140 g (5 oz) caster sugar

ground cinnamon, to serve

Method

Place rice and 300 ml (10 fl oz) water into a saucepan and simmer over a low heat until the rice is cooked and water has absorbed.

Add the milk slowly and keep stirring.

Mix the cornflour with a little water to make a paste and add to the rice mixture, together with the sugar. Keep stirring until it thickens.

When ready, pour into individual bowls and serve with plenty of ground cinnamon.

Olive Oil Yoghurt Cake with Honey Yoghurt

Serves 4 to 6

Ingredients

240 ml (8 fl oz) olive oil

150 g (5 oz) sugar

3 eggs

240 ml (8 fl oz) milk

120 ml (4 fl oz) Greek yogurt

75 g (2 1/2 oz) golden raisins

self-raising flour

zest of half orange

480 ml (16 fl oz) Greek yogurt

120 ml (4 fl oz) honey

1 teaspoon vanilla extract

Method

Preheat oven to 200°C (400°F). Pour the oil into a large mixing bowl and add the sugar. Using an electric mixer whisk together. Add the eggs, one at a time. Pour in the milk and add the yogurt, continue mixing. Add as much flour as it needs to make a smooth cake mixture. Add the orange zest and the raisins. Mix well until combined.

Pour mixture into a prepared cake tin and bake for 45–60 minutes or until skewer comes out clean when inserted.

In a medium bowl place the yogurt, honey and vanilla extract. Mix well and set aside.

Serve at room temperature or cold with honey yogurt.

For my family in Greece
who give with open
hands, thank you...

ACKNOWLEDGEMENTS

A very big heartfelt thanks to my amazing family, for all your love, support and encouragement. You know how much it means to me, you are everything.

Thank you to everyone at New Holland Publishers for saying 'yes', to Fiona, Diane, Lliane, Lesley, Jodi, Stephanie, Talina, Emma, Olga, Holly, Arlene, Yolanda, Elise and the entire creative team for your vision, creativity and enthusiasm and especially for having faith in me.

Thanks to the very gifted photographers Graeme and Greg for the exquisite photos and to the creative stylists Natasha, Stephanie and Georgie for the brilliant styling…long days spent in the kitchen and studio which were also so much fun.

Many thanks to my extended family and dear friends and of course, all the wonderful people I have met during my travels…thank you for so generously sharing recipes, stories and love of food…you all mean so much to me.

Thank you to my family in Greece, aunts, uncles and cousins who welcomed me into their homes and into their lives with open arms and hearts. Thank you, thank you, memories that will stay with me forever.

To my dear parents, you were the best.

From my heart an enormous thankyou.

Mary x

A Note from the Author

I remember the first time I went to Greece, I was a little nervous but excited at the same time. It was summer and the vegetable gardens were abundant with tomatoes, cucumbers, zucchini, greens and herbs; flowers in bloom, framing footpaths and roads – it was a delicious garden. From that very first moment, the importance of fresh, seasonal produce and a way of life became clearer to me.

Every time I go to Greece, it never fails to surprise me with the intensity of flavors in every piece of fruit or vegetable that you eat. Tomatoes so sweet, all they need is to be cut in half, drizzled with olive oil and sprinkled with a pinch of salt; salads accompanying every meal with the simplest of dressings, a drizzle of olive oil, a squeeze of a lemon and a pinch of salt; bowls of sweet cherries for dessert, or refreshing slices of watermelon.

I love the traditional recipes that are prepared all over Greece, using similar ingredients and often exactly the same but somehow a little different, depending on the hands that prepared it, of course, everyone owning their recipe as the original version.

I remember a woman saying once, 'what grows together, goes together'. Vegetables and herbs growing at the same time in the same place, picked and prepared together – the best in seasonal harmony.

The ritual every morning after breakfast was a walk to the markets to buy ingredients for the day's meal, lunch being the main meal of the day – stopping for a coffee along the way was a must.

For me, Mediterranean ingredients speak for themselves, always use the best seasonal produce you can get your hands on and prepare simply… glorious.

The Mediterranean kitchen is relaxed, seasonal and said to be the healthiest in the world.

During my travels, I have been inspired by watching families and friends gathering over long lunches, talking, laughing and enjoying food and company.

I particularly loved the small plates of food on offer - the mezethes of Greece, antipasti of Italy, hors d'oeuvres of France and the tapas of Spain. So many different tastes and, depending which country you were in, these small plates of delights and surprises were accompanied by either a glass of ouzo, wine or sangria.

Food for the body and soul.

INDEX

First published in 2019 by New Holland Publishers
London • Sydney • Auckland

Bentinck House, 3–8 Bolsover Street, London W1W 6AB, UK
1/66 Gibbes Street, Chatswood, NSW 2067, Australia
5/39 Woodside Ave, Northcote, Auckland 0627, New Zealand

newhollandpublishers.com

A record of this book is held at the British Library and the National Library of Australia.

ISBN 9781760790899

Group Managing Director: Fiona Schultz
Project Editor: Elise James
Designer: Yolanda La Gorcé
Production Director: Arlene Gippert
Printer: Toppan Leefung Printing Limited

10 9 8 7 6 5 4 3 2 1

Keep up with New Holland Publishers on Facebook
facebook.com/NewHollandPublishers

UK £14.99
US $19.99